Running on Empty
A Diary of Anorexia and Recovery

Carrie Arnold
Foreward by Susan Gottlieb, Ph.D.

First Page Publications

12103 Merriman • Livonia • MI • 48150
1-800-343-3034 • Fax 734-525-4420
www.firstpagepublications.com

Library of Congress Cataloging-in-Publication Data

Arnold, Carrie, 1980-
  Running on empty : a diary of anorexia and recovery / Carrie Arnold ;
foreward by Susan Gottlieb.
        p. cm.
  Summary: "An autobiographical account of a young woman's
struggle with and recovery from obsessive-compulsive disorder,
anorexia, bulimia and self-mutilation"—Provided by publisher.
  Includes bibliographical references.
  ISBN 1-928623-02-6
  1. Arnold, Carrie, 1980—Health. 2. Anorexia nervosa—Patients—
Biography. 3. Anorexia nervosa—Patients—Rehabilitation. I. Title.
RC552.A5A76 2004
616.85'262'0092—dc22

                                        2004024796

Cover Photography and
Design by Kimberly Franzen

To my parents,
With love and respect

Foreward

E ating disorders are devastating illnesses that affect individuals from young children to adults. Anorexia Nervosa and Bulimia Nervosa are evident in both males and females and in all socio-economic levels.

Once identified, eating disorder recovery is a difficult road. One needs to address the physical, nutritional and psychological aspects of the disease. Each of these entities carries its own challenge. For example, the person must tolerate the refeeding process which can be physically uncomfortable, while at the same time addressing the underlying issues that resulted in the eating disorder.

Recovery encompasses individual and group therapies. Also helpful are self-help books that can offer support through the entire process. *Running on Empty* is one such book. It provides powerful insight into the recovery journey. It is an honest depiction of a young woman suffering and eventually recovering from her eating disorder. The trials and tribulations are truly felt while reading this book. Hopefully it will be an inspiration to those in the pitfalls of this terrible disease and provide hope that one can recover through hard work and perseverance.

Susan J. Gottlieb, Ph.D.

Author's Statement

CR

Warning: what you are about to read actually happened. These are the events of my life, as much as they pertain to my encounter with anorexia nervosa, and the characters that populate the pages of this book are real people. Including me. I wrote *Running on Empty* as a woman in recovery from an eating disorder, my wounds still fresh from my harrowing battle that had reduced me to eighty-five pounds with one choice left: eat or die.

If I were rewrite *Running on Empty* today, two years after I declared my book 'done', the content of my story would be different – because I myself am different. Then, I was still battling. Now, I know can identify myself as a woman who has conquered. Now, when I reflect on the events that I describe in this story, my angle is different, my memories are slightly altered, and the conclusions I draw now are somewhat changed.

But I have chosen not to rewrite my story, for that would fail to affirm the person that I was at the moment I put pen to paper (or, more accurately, fingers to keyboard). Instead, I want to I acknowledge who I was in the past, while allowing for growth over time.

This is something only a reader's gentle understanding will allow, and I ask it of you now: be patient with me. I'm still growing. I'm still changing. I present to you *Running on Empty* not as a static manuscript, carved in stone, but as the dynamic, ever-changing saga of one woman coming to understand herself.

I snuffed out all other desires, and with them all other anxieties. I felt nothing but the taut pull of my stomach, throbbing with a hunger so tangible and distinct I could practically hold it in my hand.

Caroline Knapp, *Appetites: Why Women Want*

Introduction: Into the Looking Glass
Atlanta, Georgia, Summer 2001

T he shrill whine of my alarm clock marks the end of another sugar plum-encrusted journey through Candyland and my return to the land of the conscious. Another day has begun. Smacking the snooze button, I rub four hours of sleep out of my eyes and roll out of bed.

I stagger into the bathroom, pee, and stand in front of the full-length mirror for Morning Inspection. Thighs—too jiggly. Ass—oh, how wide! Belly—acceptable, if I were a pregnant woman in my third trimester. Should I start shopping in the maternity section? Damn, damn, damn. No dinner for Miss Piggy.

I rummage through my closet, pull on a pair of baggy jeans and a random T-shirt, stuff my feet into a pair of clogs, and start to brew a pot of coffee. I scrub my teeth while my magic juice percolates, and run a quick hand through my hair—nothing sticking up, fine; hurry, let's go. Can't be late for work. Where *is* that damn Sweet 'N Low? Ransacking my roommate's cupboard produces one lone packet, which I tear open and empty into the strong, dark brew. The pale pink paper flutters to the bottom of the trash can as I jam my keys into the lock after slamming the front door. My leg taps a nervous accompaniment to the morning rush-hour traffic on my commute to the smallpox labs at the Centers for Disease Control and Prevention, as my mind races ahead to what I will eat for dinner.

Keep moving, don't stop, don't ever stop, just go, dammit, go!

Take the stairs, always the stairs. I note with vague amusement the signs plastered all over the stairwell by the friendly public health educators at the CDC: each minute climbing stairs burns precisely 13.8 calories. So, I take my place at the bottom of the stairs, note the time on my watch, and ready, set, go! I jog up to the fourth floor. I am greeted by a sign that declares I have just "climbed my way to health!" Any anorexic worth her[1] stuff wouldn't be seen doing anything *but* taking the stairs.

Morning passes quickly. I refill my spill-resistant travel mug with some vile, cold Starbucks from the cafeteria. Tastes like fermented fuel oil. I pass the racks of bagels and doughnuts with hardly a second glance. Don't want those anyway, too much fat—turn you into a Mack truck.

Back in the lab, I start to OD on coffee. I wrap my trembling hands around my bony ribs to soothe the choppy sea of my churning stomach. Oh, Jesus. I heave acid and caffeine into the lab sink. God, don't let my boss walk in. How the hell do I explain all this vomit? Rinse the sink, my mouth.

Oh, I'm fine, just fine, guys, couldn't be better. How about you?

Too busy for lunch, too many papers to read. Maybe stop for some hot tea in the afternoon. Nearly insane with hunger by now. Try to focus, don't think, just don't think about it. Oink, oink, little piggy, that's what you'll be if you eat. No. I sit down with Earl Grey and "U.S. Efforts in the Eradication of the Smallpox Virus." Hmmm…how 'bout "Carrie Arnold and the Eradication of Abdominal Cellulite?"

Return to my apartment, greeted by my roommate holding a platter of warm chocolate chip cookies. She urges me to try one, a new recipe from her mom. *What do I do?* Shit. Miss Piggy takes over. I snatch the smallest one off the plate, just touching the edges. Lard is seeping into my fingers; *it is actually* touching *me*. Oh, it's good, I mumble, mouth filled with half-chewed cookie. I bolt into my bathroom, spit my mouthful into the toilet. What to do with the other half? I stuff that into my mouth, chew, and deposit that half into the bowl as well, watching the chocolatey mass swirl as I flush it away. How much damage did I do? Half ration of lettuce tonight. Make up for my gluttony. Weakling—can't even refuse a damn cookie.

---

[1] Although I refer to an anorexic as being female here, I am doing so in reference to me and don't want to cast gender stereotypes about eating disorders. At least 10% of those suffering from anorexia are male, and eating disorders should not be thought of as only "women's problems."

I change into my workout gear, a ritual far more complex than it sounds. Hop on scale, take off shoes, hop on scale, remove clothing, hop on scale, pull on Spandex, hop on scale, assemble musical gear, hop on scale, tie shoes, hop on scale. Always workout in tight clothing. More motivation. The routine is reversed after thirty minutes on the Stairmaster and twenty of jogging. Hop on scale, take off shoes, hop on scale, remove sopping clothing, hop on scale, take swig of water, hop on scale, shower (lather, rinse, repeat), hop on scale, dry off, hop on scale, put on pjs, hop on scale, pee, hop on scale.

My weight is in the "acceptable" region: five pounds less than the previous week. Special treat tonight: sugar free popsicle. I indulge in fifteen calories of artificially sweetened frozen fruit juice, *plus* an evening of gnawing on the stick. Does wood have calories? Put the stick down, Carrie.

I pluck *Betty Crocker's Best Desserts* off the bookshelf and blissfully commune with photos of gooey brownies and chocolate cake. Why can't these damned things be scratch 'n' sniff? I only want a whiff… I dash back into my room and inhale the aroma from a shoebox full of candy wrappers, the contents of which I have previously chewed and savored, then spit out. Have your cake and chew it, too.

Need to focus. Try to read articles from work, but my mind keeps wandering back to my roommate's cookies. Focus. I brew a pot of decaf.

Don't put creamer in that. Not even skim milk.

Please? I'll be good tomorrow. Promise…

No.

It's only twenty-five calories, *pretty* please?

Make up for the cookie.

Focus.

I sip the aspartame-laced potion while pacing the hallway with a fistful of articles contemplating the wisdom of destroying the remaining stores of smallpox virus. I only want to demolish the platter of cookies. Focus, focus, focus! Gluttonous cow, only thinking of chewing her cud.

Bedtime routine ensues. Five sets of twenty-five sit-ups in five different poses. Muscles tremble as I repeatedly haul my shoulders off the carpeting. Sloth. I wash my hands precisely five times, counting to fifty-five each time. After a layer of lotion coats my scaly palms, I twist the deadbolt in the front door five times to ensure everything locks properly. Set alarm, check five times.

Collapse into bed, and five rows of mustard-slathered lettuce leaves dance in my head.

❧

The mind is its own place, and in itself can make a Heaven of Hell, a Hell of Heaven.

John Milton

You could say I had it all. A loving family. Friends. High school valedictorian. Top of my college class at a small liberal arts school. Promising future in microbiology. Why would I trade all of this in for a life of torture and pain, starvation and obsession? What would drive me so blindly to heed the seductive whispers of an iniquitous voice in my head that would one day be diagnosed as anorexia?

You got me.

In some ways, I am a stereotypical anorexic; in others, I am the polar opposite. I am considered by many to be an enigma: a cloner of genes, sculptor of sentences, and phobic of pasta. I fit the profile: young, white, female, middle-class, over-achiever, obsessive-compulsive, from a close-knit family. On the surface, I'm practically a textbook example of anorexia nervosa. Yet I chafe at many of the other stereotypes of anorexics. I'm neither passive-aggressive nor a people pleaser. I don't blame everyone else's problems on myself. I remember seeing an ad for an eating disorder treatment center that summarized it rather nicely: "The behaviors? Always similar. The reasons? Never the same."

What makes my story so tragic is not its uniqueness, but how common it has become. Everyone I've talked to knows someone who has "had a bout" with anorexia or bulimia, and has seen the struggles at least secondhand. I tell my story not to elicit sympathy or pity, for I desire neither of these. Rather, I seek a deeper comprehension of both myself and this disease with which I am afflicted. A significantly warped logic pervades those with eating disorders, one that requires experience to fully understand. I routinely worked with lethal viruses with hardly a second thought, yet the thought of cream cheese set off a panic attack. I baked luscious desserts for relatives and co-workers, cutting generous portions and encouraging seconds, while simultaneously fasting for three straight days after learning that each pink packet of Sweet 'N Low had exactly two-point-five calories.

After two years of therapy and approximately half of my parents' life savings, I am no longer sick enough to be called ill, but not yet better enough to be called well. Each day takes me further away from a life once measured in pounds, calories, and sit-ups. An eerie silence replaces the endless acrobatics of compulsive calorie counting and the minute scrutiny of my rib cage to ensure that my bones do, indeed, protrude. Don't let this fool you. I still scrutinize my butt in every mirror I pass. (Is it too wide? Too round? Too flat? Too jiggly?) When I am in the fitting room at Victoria's Secret, I ask myself if it has the texture of cottage cheese. Likewise, every female I encounter gets the proverbial once-over, each body part compared to mine. Relief floods through me each time I perceive a woman to be larger than myself. Yet I am not a particularly vain person; I do not consider this obsession with my appearance to be anything *but* the eating disorder.

How could a desire to wear jeans no larger than a size zero almost prevent me from graduating college? I wish I could answer that for certain. But in the warped reality of eating disorders, few issues are ever fully resolved. There are only ideas and theories. I have come to accept that I may never know for sure what happened to me, and to some degree, that's neither here nor there.

The real question is this: how do you decide to live when you're so sure you're already dead?

CR

I became anorexic my junior year of college, although I had flirted with the disorder on and off since middle school. What astonishes me is not that I discovered anorexia, but that it took nearly twenty years for me to do so. Once I had discovered it, however, my life rapidly spiraled out of control. I was forced to leave a prestigious internship in the smallpox labs of the Centers for Disease Control and Prevention in Atlanta for an emergency hospital stay in Wisconsin. I went from six consecutive semesters on the dean's list to just another college dropout. In five months, I spent three weeks in two different hospitals and six weeks in a residential treatment center. I have lost enough.

Still, I ask myself, *is* it enough? Have I suffered enough to be rid of this disorder once and for all? Truth is, I don't know. The rational part of my mind knows that any suffering is too much, but the anorexic half would give up all that and more to be thin again. More times than I care to recall, I have had to stare at my reflection in the mirror and demand what more anorexia could want. What? *What?* I have given my job, my education, almost my life. What more is there?

I have to consciously prevent myself from finding out.

I no longer consider myself a victim of anorexia, for I refuse to play along with her twisted ploys. I didn't intend to enmesh myself in such a sadistic relationship with my reflection in the mirror, nor did I intend to abuse my body almost beyond repair. For that matter, I really didn't intend to get better. I just got tired of being sick, and, somehow, here I am. In recovery. Yet it's not one small step for anorexic-kind from "sick" to "well." There's a long in-between time where you feel your mind has split, and a mind so divided cannot stand. Logically, you know where your loyalties should lie. Do you side with the greasy Mafia boss who is trying to kill you or with the chipper cheerleader who wants you to have peace and happiness? But the choices in recovery never seem quite so simple at the time.

Since I just admitted that my book does not contain the Anorexia Recovery Answer Key, why, then, am I writing this? If I'm not writing it as an emergency flotation device for anorexics and bulimics (which I'm not), or as some form of tedious self-justification of my actions (which I hope I'm not, either), then why are you still reading? I tell my story in the hopes that someone will find strength in my weaknesses and faith in my hopelessness. I tell my story because I feel that there is something to be learned from it. Just as I hope this book will help illuminate some of the painful, confusing aspects of anorexia and recovery for you, the reader, the writing of these pages provided me with that same steady glow of light.

My goal is to describe falling into—and climbing back out of—an eating disorder as a real person experiences it. Part of what makes my story different is not that I chronicle exactly how I stumbled upon this mirror-filled nightmare called anorexia, but that I also chronicle how I'm finding my way out of this disorder. There are no storybook endings or fairy godmothers or princes on white horses. There's only me, my life, my experiences. I want to put anorexia in a spotlight that doesn't focus only on weight loss, clothing size, gossip mongering, and movie stars. I want to unveil the true face of an eating disorder, the undulating, swollen, vomit-streaked face that stares back at you from the depths of the toilet bowl water. The smooth, sunken face that moves no more and will soon be covered with dirt. Ashes to ashes, dust to dust.

Are we the fools for being surprised
That a silence could end with no sound?

Dar Williams, "When Sal's Burned Down"

All too often, the extreme calorie restriction that accompanies anorexia is described with an almost holy veneration. It is neither holy nor venerable. It is hell, a hell that threatens to dog you every step for the rest of your days. I want other people to understand how easy it is to fall into the trap of restricting and exercising, scarfing and barfing. I want others to know how long and hard and downright painful the climb is to find your way back to the world of the living.

People ask me to describe what living with an eating disorder is like. What do I describe first? The overwhelming sense of self-loathing that develops? The waves of disgust that roll over you as you stare into the mirror at your ever-shriveling body? Or how you lay in bed, night after night, shivering and restless, your starved brain unable to sleep, praying for death, but please, God, can't I be skinny first? Should I describe the heart attack that nearly ensues when you learn that each can of Diet Coke has *two whole calories* per serving? Or how, months into recovery, you still wonder if it's really okay to use low-fat sour cream instead of fat free and how, even now, you would still rather be dead than seen eating chocolate?

An eating disorder is a strange jumble of contradictions and ironies. The one thing you find to help you cope with life could very well kill you. You reject stereotypical notions of feminine curves, yet do so by embracing the culturally accepted phenomenon of dieting. Striving for perfection by starving yourself takes a sledgehammer to the very Superwoman image you hope to portray. You watch your calories like a hawk and nibble like a sparrow, this starvation sating a deep hunger in your soul. The new purpose in your life leaves you with a pointless existence.

What I did wasn't really that special. "Girl Eats Lettuce, Loses Weight" will never appear on the front of the *National Enquirer*. If I ate nothing at all and gained weight, or routinely inhaled the contents of my pantry and lost weight, well, that would be special. Losing weight by eating three hundred calories per day isn't special, it's biology. My losing fifty pounds in six months proved absolutely nothing besides the fact that my body follows the laws of biochemistry.

Was it worth almost killing myself to find this out?

Maybe.

Maybe not.

When I first let anorexia into my life, I had no idea how hard she would be to evict. I had no idea that an eating disorder didn't just go away once you were "thin." With this disease, you can always go a little further, eat a little less, exercise a little more, drop another size. You blindly put in the extra obsessive effort that just may be the final nail in your coffin because you have surrendered your life to the very thing that is trying to kill you. That this is foolhardy never occurs to you until after you have learned that anorexia fed you lies more often than you fed yourself diet pills and laxatives.

I plunged headfirst into my eating disorder, heedless of the consequences. And when I started to drown, I went down fast. Incredibly fast. No, eating disorders don't just happen, just as they don't just go away, but you can be stripped of your life (in any meaningful sense of the word) in a matter of days. Just like that. In the end, anorexia controlled not just what I ate, but every last aspect of my life. The disease robbed me of mind, body, and spirit.

Not that people didn't try to stop me. They tried. I despair at how hard they tried. But at the end of the day, when your rubbery legs exercise off the calories in five celery sticks, or you're hanging your head over the toilet, ridding yourself of half a slice of low-cal bread, help doesn't quite register with you. It doesn't mean jackshit until you are ready to accept it. Trouble is, sometimes that acceptance doesn't happen until too late, until you have a very large "Whoops..." engraved on your tombstone. I literally owe my life to the people who refused to let me go, even after I tried to get rid of them.

The twisted part was that I was convinced that my success with anorexia would make those around me writhe with envy. They writhed all right. Just not with envy. With fear. By maintaining your eating disorder, you are very literally asking your friends and family, those you love the most, to watch you die. Every day you spend entrenched in your eating disorder, you are slowly committing suicide in front of their eyes. You may honestly believe you're fine. You may think tragedy will never happen to *you*.

Treasure that thought. It may just be the last one you have.

Been saved again by the garbage truck
I got something to say you know but nothing comes
Yes I know what you think of me you never shut up
Yeah I can hear that

Tori Amos, "Silent All These Years"

Chapter One: Silent All These Years

Why would a seemingly healthy and well-adjusted young woman decide to stop eating and climb on the roller coaster of anorexia? How did she get on a ride that would bring her to the brink of death and back again? I sit here and hold the strands of my life, once woven so neatly, now a rat's nest of knots and snarls in my hands. I do not know how my life unraveled so much, so fast, nor can I comprehend how I am supposed to weave it back together. Even though I can list all sorts of attributes—genetic, cultural and otherwise—that may have contributed to my eating disorder, I can't uncover the exact reason for its development. All I can say for certain is that it sure as hell sounded like a good idea at the time. My father asked me, not all that long ago, "Why? You are so talented and smart. Why did you do this to yourself?" I wish I could answer that with certainty, for him and for myself.

Maybe there is no rationale for trying to starve myself to death, me who has been blessed with so much. Eating disorders absolutely defy logic, though these irrational actions somehow made perfect sense when I was in the midst of the mania of not eating and overexercising. Soon, I began to depend on the very thing that promised to set me free, and the eating disorder neatly plucked my life from my seemingly capable hands. But the significance of my life is not in where I have been; it lies in how far I have come since then.

I was born the second and youngest child to a pair of loving parents in West Bloomfield, Michigan, an affluent suburb of Detroit. My mother was especially delighted that her second bouncing bundle of joy was an additional source of estrogen in the house. While I did have an older brother (Kyle, by four and a half years), I tended to behave more like a spoiled only child than a brash youngest one.

As a child, I never felt I was heard, my ideas too easily brushed aside. They weren't, of course, but at age two, three, four, or ten, I thought they were. "You're not *listening!*" I would howl from the back seat of the car, on the way to a family dinner or the grocery store or wherever, indignant at being ignored for the seemingly billionth time. Tears would run down my cheeks, and I would slouch back in my seat, cross my arms over my chest, and pout, silently, for the rest of the evening. I became an expert at the silent treatment, figuring that if no one wanted to listen, then I wouldn't talk. I berated myself each time I broke down and said something to another member of my family. *Weakling*, a little voice would hiss in my brain, *absolutely no willpower.*

Little did I know how much the concept of "willpower" would come to mean to me.

From the outside, I can honestly say that my family was the shining example of the American dream—all we lacked were a dog and a white picket fence. As a family, we were hideously, grotesquely normal. Even our house blends in; to this day, I drive by and cannot find anything out of the ordinary with it, anything that would indicate that a starved person once lived inside. It's a rather ordinary-looking house on a rather ordinary-looking street. Two stories. Porch. Garage out front. No big signs proclaiming anorexia had taken up residence, though she had nonetheless. Much of my life is tied to that house. I have never moved, at least not permanently, and have always considered the gray siding and red shutters to be my place of safety and security from the menacing outside world.

I'm not indicating that *I*, personally, was normal, though no one would have ever classified me as particularly weird. I was the child perpetually praised by teachers and parents, excelling at nearly every subject I tackled, from math to music. The "Best Little Girl in the World," you could say. My classmates were generally ambivalent: half resented me for continually showing them up, half scorned my unofficial position as teacher's pet, and the remaining one or two in my class gave me a chance at friendship. On the flip side, however, I never had problems or issues with anyone or anything. I didn't drink or smoke. I didn't experiment with sex or illicit substances. I tried very hard to socially camouflage myself in order to escape the negative attention from my peers that came with having the Scholastic Midas Touch.

My childhood centered on the kitchen, and my mother's presence there. Cooking was the women's domain, a tradition handed down from mother to daughter in my family. I knew I could usually find my mom in the kitchen, and so I began to associate that room—as well as food—with love, comfort, and security. Whenever I was sad, I went to the kitchen. Whenever I was lonely, I went to the kitchen. Whenever I was angry and wanted to pick a fight, I went to the kitchen. If I wandered into the room and no one was there, I could always comfort myself with a chocolate chip cookie snagged from the ceramic rooster cookie jar.

Love, in my house, was doled out in the usual hugs and kisses, but also in the unsolicited bowls of potato chips and glasses of soda. I rarely passed an hour in my room without hearing a little tap on the door from my mom, followed by, "Can I get you some Triscuits?" Or pretzels or Cheetos or whatever. A well-fed child is a well-loved child, or so it seemed. "What can I get you to eat?" was my mother's ubiquitous question. Since "I'm not hungry" was not really an acceptable answer to someone for whom food was love, I found it easier to agree to something than protest. Special desserts were baked for birthdays and milestones, favorite meals cooked for special events. Always paying close attention to our likes and dislikes, my mom picked up surprises for us at the grocery store. To refuse food was to refuse my mother's love. To me, however, food would come to be perverted from a messenger of love—the penultimate Cupid—into a weapon of mass destruction.

And how, you might ask, did my dad fit into this system? My father and I were somewhat less close, although we got along just fine. It was just that the sex roles in my house were very explicitly divided so that my father had my brother and my mother had me. Although my father and I are currently trying to make amends for our erstwhile distant relationship by learning how to show affection for each other in a more meaningful way, his traditional way of showing love was bringing home the paycheck that put the food on the table.[2] My eating disorder symptoms proceeded to wreak havoc upon the family structure as I symbolically refused love and attention from both of my parents.

---

[2] For an insightful assessment of the impact fathers have on their daughters' eating problems, see Margo Maine's *Father Hunger: Fathers, Daughters, and Food*

On the whole, my family was pretty normal about food. No one really dieted, though perhaps some should have. Until the age of eight, I believed that a diet meant skipping the pre-breakfast cookie. Food in my house tended to be nice and orderly and fairly regimented. We ate regular meals at regular times, always having a bowl of cereal and juice for breakfast, a sandwich, fruit, and dessert at lunch, and meat, starch, vegetables, and salad for dinner. My mom cooked. My dad did the dishes. My brother and I cleaned our plates. We went out to eat pre-cisely once a week.

Eating was, in a word, a family affair. Every effort was taken to ensure that all available family members were seated together around the dinner table, which meant occasionally eating at four thirty in the afternoon or as late as eight at night. This all sounds very Pollyanna-ish, and maybe it was, but that's what became "normal" to me. When, at the age of twenty, I started avoiding mealtime in the service of my eating disorder, it was interpreted as a refusal to participate in the family unit. Short of moving out of the house, which I had neither the money nor the inclination to do, these nightly rebuffs were the stron-gest statement that could be made in my family.

Ironically, I couldn't have asked for better models of a healthy relationship with food. My dad's idea of a diet involved skipping the traditional pre-breakfast and post-dinner cookie. He never worried about fat, cholesterol, or blood pressure, figuring "don't fix what ain't broke." My mom's rationale was much simpler. "I love to eat," she would say. "I love to eat too much to ever go on a diet." We were always encouraged to take extra helpings at dinner. "Are you sure you don't want seconds, sweetie?" my mom would ask, as she dumped another spoonful onto my plate.

I grew up, in essence, loving food. My mother took great pains to ensure that we had stockpiles of groceries in the pantry—a dozen bottles of salad dressing, boxes of spaghetti piled knee deep. When I'd open the freezer, neatly wrapped packages of frozen meat would tumble out of the door. The kid in me didn't mind this in the least, especially considering that our shelves were always well-stocked with goodies. I hated going over to some of my friends' houses because I knew I would be hard pressed to find tasty treats like the ones in my house. Whereas we had several boxes of Girl Scout cookies, my friends had stale Corn Pops. It was clearly no contest. My friends and I would storm the kitchen, pull up our chairs and yell, "We're back and ready for a snack!" Around my house, it was always snack time and I frequently raided the cookie jars fifteen minutes before dinner, with only the occasional twinge of six-year-old guilt to remind me I should not be eating all this food.

As I got older, however, I began to understand that my pudginess might be somehow related to my snacking habits, and I grew to resent the perpetually filled cookie jars, even as they fueled my early morning rituals. Every Saturday morning, I would creep downstairs and filch a cookie before I had my usual bowl of cereal. I carefully lifted up the brown rooster head, reached inside, selected my treat, and silently set the head back down. At first, I was more concerned with my brother catching me red-handed and ratting on me, but by the time I was eight or nine, I independently associated eating the cookie with some sort of juvenile misdemeanor. I was committing a criminal act, and it showed in my actions. I would frantically stuff the chewy chocolate chip cookie into my mouth before anyone could see what a pig I was. Although my family had taught me it was okay to eat, the world was teaching me otherwise.

By the age of eight, I had absorbed the double standards that existed about the eating habits of men and women. Women do not eat not merely because they want to be thin. Rather, they do not eat because they are told not to hunger. Women are not supposed to want, to need, to desire anything expressly for themselves. Female lives are to be lived in service to others, quietly and meekly obeying the Diet Gods That Be. When we do give in to our strange (yet natural) cravings, we attribute our momentary weakness to PMS, pregnancy, or a relationship breakup. To anything but our bodies genuinely asking, very politely, for specific nutrients. Look in your nearest grocer's freezer and you will see Hungry Man dinners on the shelves, meals containing "One full pound of food!" Where, one might wonder, did the Hungry Woman entrees go? Women are essentially left to content themselves with Lean Cuisine and Weight Watchers. A man who eats hearty portions is a "healthy eater"; a woman who does so is a pig.

In every treatment center I have been to, I found the women curled up in the fetal position on the couches or chairs, shrinking into themselves as they tried to occupy the least amount of space humanly possible. No one ever sprawled out on the sofa. Rather, they clasped their knees to their chests and rocked, back and forth, back and forth, cramming themselves into the corners of the overstuffed furniture. I could almost hear the unspoken mantra: I am too big for this world. For most of those with eating disorders, this fear manifests itself during late childhood and into adolescence, and I was no exception.

Even at such a young age, it seemed only natural that I start to try to minimize my ever expanding body.

Summer 1988

Eight years old. We are holding a Tiffany and Debbie Gibson dance marathon in my best friend Theresa's basement.

"I'm hungry," I report. She shrugs her shoulders and leads me into her kitchen. She opens the refrigerator door.

"We have carrots."

"Yuck." I wrinkle my nose. "Doesn't your mom have anything *good*?"

"Of *course* she does." Theresa rummages through the freezer, producing a squashed carton of chocolate ice cream. She pries the lid open and peers in—only a spoonful left. She replaces the box. "We could chew on ice cubes."

"Ice cubes?" I stare at her spindly limbs. I suddenly realize why she is so skinny—they never have anything to eat around her house. I silently wish my house didn't have so many cookies and cupcakes. Then I could be thin, too. I abruptly decide to go on a diet. "Okay."

We each take several cubes, tossing the extras from hand to hand as we chew and slurp, water dripping off our chins and making dark tracks down our T-shirts. "Yum," I say. "Fills you up." My stomach growls noisily, a noticeable contrast to what I had just said. I pretend I didn't hear it. Soon, the Bangles' "Walk Like an Egyptian" drowns out the complaints from my empty stomach. All thoughts of dieting are soon forgotten.

My mom comes to drive me home, and once I step through our front door I make a mad dash for the cookie jar. I cram Oreos into my mouth, one after another, desperate to fill up the empty hole of my stomach. I remember, suddenly, my vow to go on a diet. I stop cold and stare at the cookie crumbs in my hand. I have failed. I couldn't even diet for two hours. *Fatso...* I shrug and continue eating. My eight-year-old brain simply figures that if you're going to break your diet, you may as well *really* break it. *You'll always be fat. Just accept it.*

So I did.

It was something I was used to accepting, even at that age. Two years earlier, at my sixth birthday party, I remember, very distinctly, that all of my new clothes were size 6X. That my clothing size was now larger than my age absolutely horrified me, because none of the other girls I knew wore clothes *that big*. I felt huge. I was deeply envious of all of my stick-thin friends who didn't have to look for clothes with pleats and tucks. I resigned myself to a life of fat and misery, of dowdy knee-length skirts. "It's more flattering to your thighs that way," my mother would gently explain. Oh. I get it. I have fat thighs. Other girls could wear "slim-fit" pants and leggings and things without pleats. No matter how frequently my mother would kindly reassure me otherwise, I understood my body parts to be larger than every other girl my age. Even at age six, I knew I took up more space than society allowed.

By the end of my elementary school years, I was beginning to do what is commonly referred to as "developing." My father slowly but surely became aware that (surprise!) his daughter was maturing, and found the concept completely baffling. In fifth grade, he sat me down with something "very important" to tell me.

"I think you (mumble) training bra (mumble mumble)."

"*What* did you say?"

"I *said*, I think it's about time you started wearing a bra."

"But why?"

"Because… well… you, um, jiggle. Just a bit." My father's face was beet red as he stared at something absolutely intriguing on the toe of his tennis shoe.

I fought wearing a bra because none of my friends did, and I really didn't think it necessary. Plus, Ryan from my class spent his recess snapping Kelly's bra straps (the only other girl in my class who had sprouted boobs), and I hated the idea of running from him almost as much as I hated running in general. I eventually lost the bra battle, but managed to work out a cease fire agreement that only required me to wear one on days when I wore a white T-shirt. So my mom and I went to Sears, and I tried on all different sizes of junior miss bras, my face practically igniting from mortification the whole time.

"Which one do you like the best?"

"I hate all of them," I whined from inside the fitting room.

"Well then, which one do you hate the least?"

I walked out with a standard white bra (size 32AA) and a pink sports bra. I cursed God for giving me breasts. Ironically enough, I am fairly flat-chested today, even though I developed earlier than most of my classmates. Some people speak longingly of a cute, curvaceous C cup; I'd settle for a cute, curvaceous A. Truth be told, I enjoy having no breasts. I'd rather be flat as a pancake than carry jugs my whole life—all they did was bounce around. Though, at the time, I feared my breasts would expand exponentially with my age and eventually get so huge I would fall over forwards.

I hated puberty. Not that anyone really completes this time in his or her life and says "Hey! That was fun! Let's do it again!", but I especially hated this phase, due in large part to the fact that I was progressing through the changes of puberty much faster than my classmates. I looked so different on the outside, but on the inside, I was the same young, insecure Carrie.

Though my parents tried valiantly to raise their children with a healthy sense of self-respect, they also never demonstrated their own human infallibility. My father was never wrong. Ever. He always had all the answers and did everything right. If something failed, it certainly wasn't his fault, because he was perfect. My mother, on the other hand, was Supermom. She kept an immaculate house, so immaculate that she complained of "lowering her standards" when she stopped ironing all of our pillowcases. She always had us kids fed and looking picture perfect. She never failed at this, never once flopped out on the couch and said, "The hell with cooking! Let's go out tonight."

Growing up, I didn't see two parents trying to do their best for their children. I didn't see them easily tolerating mistakes in others. Through my child eyes, I only saw this: Messing Up is not an option. Failure is not tolerated. Perfection is the minimum we expect. In my eyes, nothing I did was ever good enough, and it was impossible to live up to these edicts of perfection. If I got one answer wrong on a tough homework assignment, I didn't feel pride for a job well done. Instead, I spent the evening berating myself for that one mistake, seeing only the big red "X" on the page rather than the "99" circled at the top. And, on the off chance I found myself satisfied with my work, I immediately raised the bar, pooh-poohing my latest achievement and setting my standards ever higher.

This sense of imperfection and impending failure developed first and most notably in my schoolwork, and grew almost frenzied with the introduction of the grade-point average in middle school. However, at the same time, another number became increasingly important to me, especially as my body changed from a girl to a woman. I became a born-again scale worshipper. Just as I found my GPA malleable, I was discovering that my appearance and my weight were, too. And so I set out on an adolescent crusade to shed my pounds of imperfections and show the world a Carrie free from even the slightest flaws.

I was tired of being told to wear loose-fitting clothes that would "flatter my figure" or minimize the size of certain body parts. "Don't wear print pants," my mother would sagely advise. "They make your thighs look bigger." She did this with the best of intentions; it was the outside world that wanted to cram me into a supermodel mold. I soon came to the conclusion that if I could just drop some of this baby fat, then I would be pretty and happy and popular. Then I could wear stretch leggings with print flowers on them just like the other middle school girls who so obviously had it all together.

Our culture tries to lead us on a search for our "inner thin person," that lean and happy other-self trapped in our self-induced flabby misery. We think SlimFast peddles "energy bars" and gritty shakes to help us deflate our spare tire; what they're trying to sell is happiness in a can. If only we could be thinner, lose five pounds, or stretch our current weight over a taller frame, then all the happiness in the world would knocking at our door. In my adolescent daydreams, I always imagined myself as being slender and graceful, a perfect size six, a girl who could wear a bikini in public and have people sigh, "If only I could have her body." It was bliss.

By the time I was twelve, I had discovered the world of dieting. Up became down and down became up. Myself and everything I represented were boiled down to a number on a scale. This meant I was continually staring at my face in the mirror, pinching my chubby cheeks. I would turn sideways and examine my stomach from every possible angle, stretching my sweatshirt down to my knees. I wondered if other girls had a poochy stomach. I realized mine stuck out much farther than anyone else I knew—except for my pregnant cousin, who was ready to pop any day now. "Can't you see how *huge* this is? Look at how it sticks out. *Look at it!*" I shrieked to my mother, on the verge of tears. I then practiced saying, "No, thank you. I'm full," to my politely smiling reflection in the mirror, each time trying to stretch the truth a little further into the guise of believability.

I put my new skills to the test approximately one week later at a seasonal piano recital, of which I was the dubious star. These musical galas consisted largely of runny-nosed five-year-olds whacking out "Twinkle, Twinkle Little Star," and "Old MacDonald Had A Farm," the children of parents trying to broaden the horizons of their off-spring. I sat in the back, bored, waiting my turn and contemplating the broadness of my thighs. I wore a cream-colored sweater, hunter green corduroy shorts ("They really flatter your figure," my mother had told me as I paraded around the fitting room), matching green tights, black flats. After the music, the snack bar. I drooled in anticipation of the long line of goodies. Usually, I would load my napkin with cookies and brownies and cheerfully munch my way through the rest of the afternoon. But this time, I slapped my hand as it came to rest on the mountain of brownies. *Stop it, PIG.* Instead, I filled a little Dixie cup with water and sipped while everyone else enjoyed the feast. *Only pigs eat junk food, and I am* not *a pig. Not anymore.* I nibbled at a carrot stick. "See?" I told my parents proudly. "I'm eating my vegetables."

"That's nice, but don't you want something else?"

"Nope. I'm on a diet." I demonstrated my newfound self-control by not even touching a single cookie.

"Don't be ridiculous," my mom reassured me. "You don't need to lose weight. You have a nice figure just as you are."

This was the crux of the problem. I did not *want* the "nice figure" or shapely thighs or round hips that my mother and her generation so obviously admired. Most pubescent girls dipping their toes into the swirling adolescent waters tend to grow up, and then out. I did the precise opposite. My weight jumped a few years before my height had a chance to catch up, and I was acutely aware of this fact while I was waiting.

I remember an episode, at the age of eleven, where my mom tried to dress me in red stretch pants. "I LOOK LIKE A BOB EVANS SAUSAGE IN THESE!!" I yowled indignantly from my room, refusing to open the door and be seen. "Don't you know that I'm just *too fat* for this type of pants?" I demanded of my mother. She tried to reassure me. "You have a womanly figure, dear." Well, I could *see* that. How could I explain that I didn't *want* a womanly figure, and would prefer to have nothing to do with curves? But, little by little, curves I slowly got, and no amount of hoping and wishing reduced them to their pre-pubescent shape.

> Rosie looked at herself in the mirror all the time now, half to see how she looked, half to make sure she was really there. She saw in the mirror the world's saddest person. When she was eleven, she used to look in the mirror and imagine herself in the movies. Now, at thirteen, she saw herself all of a sudden as she imagined others saw her. Late at night, very late, when she explored the dark dangerous existential place where sleeplessness took her, she'd traipse down the hall to the bathroom, and look at her weird sick face in the medicine chest mirror. Under the awful humming lights she could see how other she was, could see the wrinkles and bumps and pores.

Anne Lamott, *Crooked Little Heart*

November 1992

For a twelve-year-old in a desperate search for independence, it was the chance of a lifetime—a day of Christmas shopping at the mall without adult supervision. After months of pleading to browse unsupervised with some girlfriends, I finally had my chance. Though my friends from school might not have realized it, I also met someone new at the mall that day, a stern, demanding companion who would return home with me and rule my life for more than a decade.

Since Theresa, my best friend and dance partner of years past, was to be returning home in a few months from a temporary move to Florida, I was determined to maintain my weight somewhere in the neighborhood of one hundred pounds. I wanted finally to be thin like her. I wanted her to be proud of me. And my twelve-year-old brain, half-inebriated on surges of estrogen, was honestly convinced I could reduce myself by thirty pounds in the space of a month. A trip to the mall, out of my mother's relentless supervision and well-intentioned food shovel, was the perfect time to start my diet.

At Sbarro's Pizzeria that day, I realized that a humongous slice of lipid-laden pepperoni pizza with puddles of grease I could swim in was clearly far more than I needed. A simple bowl of salad was much more adequate. I grilled the acne-faced teenaged boy behind the counter about the salad dressing, and when I learned that nothing fat free existed, I opted for no dressing at all. Now, I am not a rabbit, nor do I particularly desire to eat like one. But I dutifully nibbled at my lettuce, taking long swigs of my diet soda between bites to wash the taste of, well, nothing out of my mouth.

See? I didn't need to eat.

Don't let anyone know what you did. They'll just be jealous. Wait. Patience, my child. One day, we'll show them. We'll show them all.

Helga had spoken.

I named this voice in my head, the seductive whisperer, the drill sergeant, and the envy of the worst of Hitler's SS Guards—Helga. I envisioned her as a very large, tank-like, gray-haired woman in wire-rimmed spectacles, one who beats me with a stick for wanting strudel. She never formally introduced herself to me (how rude), instead just invited herself into my head and moved in, whereupon she began to order me around. And I obeyed. Of course, Helga wasn't all Nazi bitch. She could be subtle, an oily, smooth charmer, winning me over with promises of impending glory and improved self-control. Once she had her hooks in, though, all niceties disappeared and I was alone in Nazi boot camp.

Both Helga and the hollowness in my gut stayed with me while I simultaneously browsed and dodged crowds of howling children waiting to tell their deepest wishes to Santa. I don't honestly remember what gifts I bought or where I found them that day, but I can still feel the numbness that followed me around the mall and back into my house as I picked at my dinner of a plain baked potato (hold the sour cream and butter, please). I countered the incessant growling in my gut all evening with bottles of Diet Faygo Raspberry Crème Soda.

I recently ran across my journals from this time, and saw that I had scribbled page after page chronicling each diet I was on, my vows to avoid sweets, my dreams of being thin. I would inspect my reflection in the mirror every day, taking note of each despised body part—thighs, hips, stomach, boobs—and try to exercise the excess away. Caroline Knapp writes that this separation of mind and body is "a way of coaxing the eye outward instead of inward, of learning to experience the body as a thing outside the self, something a woman *has* rather than something she *is*."[3]

In my thirteenth year, I began in earnest to experiment in the field of weight loss. I refused to eat anything but turkey sandwiches at school, dissecting one half while I nibbled on the other. I would go all day on half a bagel, ripping up the other half and flushing it down the toilet. I recorded and bragged in my journal of how little I'd eaten, my childish handwriting scrawling down the page as I underscored the important parts. "I had only one half grapefruit so far today, it's dinnertime, and I'm *not even hungry!!!*" I was lying about not being hungry, of course. In reality, I wanted to rip out some of the pages from the back of my journal and chew on those for a little while.

Restricting became a lifestyle, and my new companion, Helga, cheered me on all the while. I genuinely believed that losing weight would make all my imperfections and insecurities just disappear into thin air. While I was on my extremely limited diet, I found myself compelled to exercise religiously, garnering more than a few questions from my mother. "Aren't you taking this whole exercise thing a little too far?" she would ask. "You're fine just the way you are." I would answer, "No, no, of course I'm not taking this too far." How can you possibly take a diet too far? Helga silently chimed in, *You think* this *is far? You just wait! You just wait and see! We'll show you how far you can take a diet.*

---

[3] Knapp, pg. 96.

My mom watched a lot of *Oprah*, and so entertained me with all sorts of sordid tales about what would happen if I didn't shape up my eating. I remember watching an episode on teens with anorexia, and I was enthralled. I thought it was just *so awesome* that these girls didn't have to eat and they were skinny and everyone was jealous of them. *You can be that thin, too*, Helga buzzed in my ear. I began to study every article on eating disorders I could find. I scoured *Seventeen* and *YM* for articles like "I Survived an Eating Disorder," using the gory tell-all stories as advice manuals. Anorexia sounded like the answer to all my problems and I was chomping at the bit to give it a try myself. To me, anorexics had it all figured out. They knew what they wanted, they went after it, and to hell with everyone else. Or so I thought.

I also began to read about girls who made themselves throw up in an attempt to lose weight. Hmmm... there was an idea that hadn't occurred to me. I filed it away in the back of my head in the event of an emergency. One arose sooner than I anticipated, during my family's weekly Sunday brunch pancake binge. I selected two from the stack, cut them up into itty-bitty pieces, and sprinkled powdered sugar over the top. I asked myself, is it really okay to have powdered sugar when you're on a diet? Helga must have thought so, and soon a sugary blizzard enveloped my plate. I wiped up every last white flake with my mini pancake-sponges, scraping my plate clean.

"Don't you want another one?" my mother asked, heaping two or three more onto my plate. "You didn't really have that much."

Did I break down? I did. I confessed: Father, forgive my weakness, give us not this day our daily bread. I wolfed down two more pancakes, my half-empty stomach skipping over the requisite toppings. Then, I panicked. What had I done? What had I just *done*? I ran upstairs to the bathroom, yanked the toilet seat up, tried to barf. I couldn't. Desperation—*do something you fat pig. Just* barf, *dammit!* I seized my toothbrush, jammed it down my throat. Nothing happened. What was *wrong* with me? Why wouldn't my body function the way it was supposed to? Chagrin flooded my stomach. I had to get rid of this food. Desperate, I tried one last time. I barfed up approximately one pancake.

It was something.

That your body isn't supposed to be violated in this manner hadn't yet occurred to me. It was the whole *not* puking part of this episode that struck me as unnatural, not the gagging myself with a toothbrush. After that, I decided the whole throwing up thing just wasn't for me. My body just wouldn't cooperate.

All of this dieting over the year I was thirteen had produced a weight loss of approximately fifteen pounds. To the average dieter, fifteen pounds is no small accomplishment. But to an obsessive perfectionist who could lose fifteen pounds and immediately find herself compelled to lose twenty more, it was a drop in the bucket. Discouraged and unhappy, I made a grudging, tentative peace with my stomach, thighs, and butt. I simply accepted that I would always be overweight, awkward, and unpopular.

For a time, it worked. For a time, Helga let me forget.

ଔ

Until the year preceding the development of my full-blown eating disorder, I was never systematically neurotic about food like I was at age thirteen. Even now, I look back to try and figure out what happened, why my eating changed back to abnormal again. I had banned potato chips in high school, started cutting down on the pizza in college. More and more foods were gradually added to the *Verboten* list. The problem with anorexia is that it starts in a series of baby steps. One forbidden food here, another set of leg lifts there, and so on. Individually, these "food rituals" are affectations, nothing more. Together, they can become a disease. Every time you eliminate a food, you feel a power surge. *Yes. I am in control here.* But by the time you realize you are living on apples and carrot sticks, you have tied yourself in a huge knot and you can't figure out how to loosen the bonds, even if you want to.

Anorexia is a cunning enemy. She works silently, stealthily, equally capable in college dormitories, tiny apartments, and sprawling mansions. She lurks within the shadow of the familiar and acceptable, from the exercise queen to the health nut, concealing her true nature behind an innocent exterior. Dangling in front of your eyes, an eating disorder casts the bait and waits for you to swim forward and take the hook. You, all high and mighty, don't even see it coming, and would refuse to believe it even if you did. From there, all she has to do is reel you in, her promises blossoming in the sweet spring air. *Yesssssss...* a voice whispers in your ear. *Thinner... then you'll be happy. Thinnerrrrrr...*

And so you are caught, ensnared in a deadly game, the outcome of which will determine the course of your life.

Want you to hear what I have to say,
live with a fear that'll scare you away.
I silently keep the pain deep inside,
wait for the day that I won't have to hide.

Tony Medina, "Out of My Mind"

Chapter Two: Out of My Mind

It struck like a kick in the gut.

My carefully constructed childhood reality crumbled one snowy December day during my freshman year in high school. In that single moment, you could say, I grew up. No longer did my days pass in carefree bliss and ignorance. Gone were the illusions of invincibility. From that time forward, the world loomed over my shoulder, ever present, ever threatening.

Our health class was watching a video on HIV and STDs, my attention wandering in and out, when something suddenly went *clunk* in my mind. I panicked and my brain raced ahead of me, obsessed with and possessed by the recurring thought that I could have AIDS, *I could be HIV-positive right here right now and not even know it.* Worse, I could pass this death sentence on to my family and friends. I immediately ran to the girls' bathroom, my stomach churning, and heaved up my lunch from earlier that day.

Breathe. I tried to will my thundering pulse into silence. Calm. Breathe. You're okay. It's all okay. Breathe. My heartbeat slowed to a gentle canter, but a terrible, sickly feeling still clutched and clawed at my stomach, an insistent reminder that something was not quite right. So I did the only thing I could think of—I washed my hands several times in hot, soapy water and went back to class.

But the terror stayed rooted in my mind. Sometimes, it elbowed its way to the front of my thoughts and overrode everything else. At other times, it droned annoyingly in the background, the evasive buzzing fly you can neither ignore nor swat. I couldn't stop thinking about how my very presence was a death sentence to those around me.

In order to alleviate these fears, I began to wash my hands more frequently. At first, it was a joke for my father and brother at the dinner table— "Oh, look! Carrie's *so* filthy!"—but soon it deepened and became more troubling. I could hardly go five minutes without washing, and before long, simple soap was no longer good enough. I needed bleach, ammonia water, Soft Scrub. My raw, cracked, and bleeding hands had fallen victim to my all-consuming compulsion to clean myself and feel, for the thirty seconds after I had finished scrubbing, normal for once.

I was aware of what obsessive-compulsive disorder (OCD) was, of course, though I believed the disorder referred to unreasonable fears and rituals. My fears of AIDS and other germs and diseases, you see, were completely realistic to me. To anyone else, it was obvious that there was no possible way I could have AIDS, but I always feared the freak chance of fate that would make me HIV-positive. And it was these fears that would come to govern my life. I was terrified at the thought of having to give up my hand washing, because I felt it was the only thing that stood between me and certain death. I knew my behavior was not normal, though I thought it perfectly rational. Yet I worried so constantly that sleeping became a fond memory, and I stopped enjoying even the simplest of things, slumping into a deep depression.

Signs that I was dying of AIDS began to surface everywhere I looked. My weight started to plummet because I had virtually no appetite, and what I did eat didn't tend to stay down. I frequently awoke from terrifying dreams, pajamas clinging to my limbs as I lay in bed, drenched in a cold sweat. The "evidence" piled up. And still I washed. I eventually discovered antibacterial hand gels. They stung terribly on my chapped skin, like wave after wave of pricks from a hundred large-gauge needles, but it loosened my anxiety. Just a little. Just a bit. Just enough to enable me to physically go through the motions of life.

Even my dreams weren't safe. I tossed and turned all night, trying to decide how I was going to break the terrible news to my parents— their daughter was dying of AIDS. And if she wasn't, she was certainly losing her mind. Which was worse? I would lay there, paralyzed by fear, unable to move. Was I dying? Or just crazy?

I feared I was both.

After several months, other people began to notice my preoccupation with washing and germs. My mother warned me, "I hope you're not getting that obsessive-compulsive thing." I flatly denied it. This was a life-and-death matter, not a psychiatric illness. I never kept track of how many times per day I would traipse over to the sink, turn the water on scalding hot, and suds up, though it was enough to cause my hands to become perpetually red, raw, and chapped. I would hum to myself as I washed in an attempt to measure precisely how long I had scrubbed, so I would know when I was "clean." If I lost count halfway through, I had to start washing all over again; a scrubbing session that lasted even *one second* less than it should was entirely worthless and had to be redone.

This OCD-induced tailspin made me become almost manic—hyper-alert to my surroundings, gaze wandering everywhere, attention landing nowhere. My mind whirred in constant motion, spurred on by terror, worry, and childlike fears. And, in case you were wondering, distractions didn't work. Not that I didn't try, but I also lived with the sinking suspicion that *I am dying right here as we speak*, and I could not, *could* not, forget about it. Reading a book, watching TV, or flipping idly through a catalogue all failed to occupy my mind fully enough to divert my attention from the all-absorbing melodrama unfolding in my head. Every now and then, however, my little tricks worked, and I was blessed with a few seconds of peace. But the moment I realized that, for the first time in a month, anxiety wasn't forcing dinner out of my stomach and my mind was free and clear, all of it ended. Reality returned with a resounding clatter, and my hard-earned serenity scampered away. I took my place once more in the world of terror, germs, and disinfectants.

OCD slowly tightened its grip on my life as spring melted into summer the year I turned fifteen. Had I not been forced to maintain the façade of normality, I know I wouldn't have left the house. Silverware at restaurants had been touched by countless workers, T-shirts in the store had passed through any number of hands, and fellow teens surely harbored several STDs each. The world was not safe for me, and I very much wanted to hide.

"You don't need to be worrying about that," my mom told me when I vaguely mentioned something about feeling dirty. "There's nothing to be afraid of." This only confirmed my deepest fears, that no one really understood how grave the situation was. Thing was, the situation *was* grave, but in a way I never would have imagined. As my current therapist regularly reminds me, if I would have been diagnosed with OCD in high school and started on Prozac[4] then, it is unlikely that the eating disorder would have ever developed. It certainly would have saved my family and me a lot of grief and suffering.

My angst was redoubled during the time I spent babysitting for a number of neighborhood children. Here the parents were, innocently thinking that they were hiring a normal babysitter, when in waltzes an HIV-positive, disease-infested, germ-ridden killing machine. I made sure to touch as little of the house as I could and scrubbed my hands with an extra fierce intensity. I remember, with exquisitely painful clarity, the concern in my five-year-old charge's voice as she asked me about my frequent trips to the bathroom. "Carrie? Why are you always going to the potty?" she asked, her brow furrowed in concentration at the coloring book page in front of her. "What do you do in there?" How could I explain the kick of anxiety that literally left me breathless and gasping for air? How could I tell her that her house was downright filthy, and so was everything else in this world? I couldn't. Instead, I made up stories about not feeling well, my tummy hurt, I had spicy food for dinner, anything that might explain my frantic flight to the bathroom every five minutes. I eventually gave up trying to explain and just told her I had to pee an awful lot. She found the word "pee" extremely funny and let the subject drop. It soon became apparent that an OCD-ridden world does not even qualify as a shell of a life. The incessant anxiety began to extract a sharp toll, costing me my happiness and, bit by bit, my sanity. I was so miserable, I wanted to swallow a bottle of Advil and have it bloody *done* with already. But even death was forbidden to me—I feared I might give some strange disease to the coroner, bearing the responsibility for not only my own death (which I could handle), but also that of an innocent bystander (which I couldn't). I had no way out. Trapped in my own life.

My contamination fears rapidly overran every aspect of my life. I used passing time at school to bolt to the girls' room and at least rinse off my hands, if not completely scrub them down in scalding hot water. "What are you *doing* in there?" my friends would ask. "Don't you feel well?" Panic seized me. You could only eat bad Chinese takeout so many times before people caught on that there were no rotten little

---

[4] Prozac is part of a class of anti-depressant drugs called Selective Serotonin Reuptake Inhibitors (SSRIs) that work in the brain to increase the amount of serotonin, a neurotransmitter. A low level of serotonin has been associated with depression, anxiety/OCD, and eating disorders, thus making me something of a Prozac Poster Child.

cartons of fried rice and egg rolls. They were getting too close to finding out the real truth—their classmate had finally gone over the edge. The urge to protect these rituals of mine eventually outweighed the need to perform the rituals themselves. I can't precisely explain why, but I eventually came to the realization that either I was going to have to go public with my hand washing, so to speak, or I would have to rid myself of this habit.

I had to stop washing. So I did.

Of course, it was neither that straightforward nor that easy. In the interim, I found myself unable to pay attention to my teachers or complete my classwork. My mind stayed frozen on the multitude of bacteria that were growing all over my body. Germs were *tainting* everything I *touched*, how could people *stand* to live in such *filth*? I found excuses to go wandering through the hallways, stopping to stand in front of the ladies' room door, wondering how people could walk past a sink and *not wash*. Heart beating a veritable drumroll in my chest, I forced air in and out, in and out, with deep, ragged breaths. Sweat beaded on my upper lip and my hands trembled as I forced my legs to continue on past the door of the bathroom. On days when I was feeling particularly brave, I (gulp) forced myself to (gulp) touch the stall door (gulp gulp).

I learned later that I had stumbled upon the classic method used in the treatment of OCD, known as exposure and response prevention. This is where you knowingly expose yourself to the things that cause anxiety, and then you refrain from doing the compulsive behavior that leads to relief. So, if you fear germs, you touch things you think are "dirty" and then don't allow yourself to wash. In the case of eating disorders, where you compulsively count calories, you would eat a lunch, then refuse to let yourself calculate the caloric total. This whole process essentially floods your anxiety defenses so that, after a while, what used to send you into a tailspin will hardly ruffle your feathers.

My triumph with this method was my first moment of *ennui* in years. For once my mind was not occupied with thoughts of my own funeral, and I had no idea what to do with the stillness in my head. I still showered and washed my hands after I used the bathroom, but I hadn't neurotically washed or obsessed about dirt for two whole days.

My OCD didn't just "go away" when I got the hand washing under control. It mutated, taking on a life of its own, and it manifested itself in various areas of my life. For a couple of months, I was so terrified that I had struck an animal, or worse, a pedestrian, with my car that I would circle the block, double checking to make sure that no dead bodies lay in the road. I watched every edition of the local news to see if there had been any reports of hit and run accidents. Later, I had difficulty writing in my journal because my handwriting wasn't perfect enough. Even the smallest flaw would cause such anxiety that I would rewrite whole pages. I started fixating on the number five, which I still do to this day, feeling somehow safe and secure in the knowledge that whatever is in front of me can be easily divided into five different portions. But thankfully these weren't all-consuming like the germs, AIDS, and hand washing had been. I was a bird let out of her cage, free to fly wherever she chose. Only this bird had clipped wings and could never quite get off the ground.

CR

In response to my partial freedom from OCD, I found my life had a terrible emptiness to it, a gaping maw I tried to fill any way I could. Some people turn to drugs or alcohol or food. Not me. Instead, at the age of sixteen, I became a workaholic, desperately trying to distract myself from the doldrums of everyday life. The twisted part about being a young workaholic was how often I was commended for making my life a living hell. The rewards were ripe for the picking, and were also, ironically enough, virtually identical to the ones I would reap by nearly starving myself to death.

Both teachers and students were always astonished when they heard of the long hours of studying I put in for each exam, or the exquisite care with which I placed every last comma in an essay. Looking back, I suppose this came as no surprise to those who really knew me, but the alacrity with which I did my work was nonetheless the cause of much disbelief, if not envy. "How the hell are you still *standing?*" they asked, amazed that I was still capable of functioning at all, let alone decently. "Don't you get *tired?*" It was, in my mind, very simple. Don't think about it. In fact, don't think at all. I kept going more by virtue of momentum than by any superhuman qualities I had somehow acquired. I ran myself ragged with my endless studying, on top of my jobs at both the library and as a babysitter. I woke up early on the weekends and stayed up late into the night working during the week, snatching only a few minutes here and there to curl up with a book or chat with friends over coffee.

I tell you this not to elicit pity about my former life or because I particularly care that you know what I did every weekend (which would make a boring story, besides), but because I want to emphasize the parallels between my obsessive studying in high school and college and my eventual collision with anorexia. It's all part of the same messy, snarled ball of yarn that is my life. I have a long and rather extensive history of using obsessive thoughts and compulsive behaviors, be it studying or starving, to cope with life. Essentially, my eating disorder is simply one more branch of this OCD-tree.

During high school, my GPA rocketed almost off the charts and I wound up, not surprisingly, at the top of my class. I endured my high school graduation as valedictorian with all of the usual hoopla, and found myself heading off to Hope College, a small Christian liberal arts school in western Michigan. Before moving away my freshman year, I vowed to maintain my 4.0 grade point throughout college, regardless of the effort involved. For the first year, I was successful. My quest for perfection, however, came at a fearful cost. I surrendered my happiness in exchange for all As, a trade whose end result left me even more vulnerable to the seductive whispers of anorexia.

My freshman year at Hope was marked, most noticeably, by my first thorough dunking into the ocean of depression. My previous experiences with depression were completely related to my OCD. Prior to this time, when my anxieties had subsided, so did the feelings of hopelessness about my life. This time around, however, it was completely different as I floundered my way around campus. I started my freshman year with sophomore standing, and I found my classes (advanced calculus and organic chemistry, to name a couple) overwhelming. I thought myself inadequate for college life.

Besides the strong biochemical component, I think my issues stemmed, in part, from the fact that I put too many expectations into my college experience. I thought college would be perfect, that I would have enough time to get straight As and have an active social life. I thought I would instantly meet tons of like-minded people and form lifelong friendships. It didn't quite happen that way. In truth, I was stuck in a shoebox-sized room with someone who was also struggling with depression, and it was not a good combination.

On the surface, my life looked wonderful by the second semester of my freshman year—I had good grades, a job editing the features section of the *Anchor* (Hope's student newspaper), and a promising summer research position in a biology lab—everything a person could ask for. I should have been happy, not hopeless and restless. The "should" business ate at me the most. I could handle not being chipper all the time, but not when my friends from high school seemed to be having the time of their lives.

My e-mails and phone calls home grew terse and strained, an unusual situation for me, as my parents and I usually got along pretty well. My mother, in particular, liked to keep abreast of things as they were happening in my life, so that she could lend support where I needed it. Psychologists and experts place an enormous emphasis on the mother/child relationship, and this was especially important in my case. A number of my friends would describe themselves as being close to their mothers, but I took "close" to something of an extreme. There comes a point when two people are so close that their concept of self is lost and they become enmeshed in each other. You cannot say for sure where one person ends and the other begins. The relationship becomes toxic, unhealthy, because your own sense of self cannot develop when it is all tied up in the identity of the other person. I was very uncertain about who I was at this point in my life, and my mom, always overprotective, never pushed me to take a leap and explore the world beyond my immediate family. For both of us, it was safer to stay within the close confines of the family structure than to begin developing as individuals.

> The mothers of anorexics are… typically talented women who sacrificed their own ambitions and careers in the service of their families… What makes the whole situation particularly explosive is that in the contemporary environment adolescent girls are everywhere surrounded by an ideology of independence, an ideology that can often induce its own feelings of guilt and inadequacy for not being able to 'break away.' This poses a particularly painful dilemma for the girl who becomes anorexic, who tends to feel a poignant sense of responsibility for her mother's well-being.[5]

Anorexia tends to present itself first during adolescence, when the future anorexic begins to pull away from the mother-child dyad. She tries to form her own, independent modality and, essentially, fails. Even though adolescence had ended for me in terms of calendar years, my development into an autonomous person had been delayed for a variety of reasons, the main one being the virtual arrest of my social development with the onset of OCD. I developed a deep-seated fear of anyone outside my immediate family and two close friends. Every-

---

[5] Gordon, pg. 103

one else just disappointed or hurt me in the end, so I wouldn't let myself trust anyone. I didn't form any sort of support system outside of my nuclear family and so remained very much a child in everyone's eyes. Exploration of relationships outside of the family circle was distinctly discouraged (the family, after all, had to come first), though not necessarily forbidden, which led both my brother and me to stay rather close to home.

> The mother is reluctant to let her daughter go (for the mother herself may be merged with her daughter out of her own lack of having a separated self), and the daughter herself has not yet embodied a sufficient sense of self to separate... Detachment from the family and realignment with peers involves tension and distress. Just as... separation is desired on one level, the wish to stay close and 'protected' within the well-known psychic ambience is in conflict with the desire for separation and autonomy.[6]

While I was able to separate intellectually from my mother, I was unable to do so in the emotional sense. Even from a very young age, my emotional development has suffered at the hands of my intellect, and the case was no different here. Both my mother and I were unable, it seemed, to loosen the ties that bound us together. Just as one of my mother's main jobs was to take care of me, I appointed myself caretaker of her. For as long as I can remember, I saw how closely her happiness intertwined with mine, and I took it onto my shoulders to ensure that she stayed that way.

What happened was this—I didn't like being a child, and saw adulthood as my salvation. During my freshman year of college, I threw myself headlong into the adult world and found myself ill-equipped to deal with life on my own. I realized that I preferred the security and comfort of life as a child, that maybe I wasn't as worldly as I would have liked to believe. A deepening chasm formed between the life I had envisioned for myself and the one I was living, and from that void, Helga emerged victorious once more. My obedience to Helga was my attempt, however warped and pathological, to grow up. I thought that if I could just stop being so damned *needy* all the time, then I would have some magical, happy Barbie doll life, replete with my own

---

[6] Orbach, pgs. 26-7

tall and handsome Ken, and scads of skinny, scantily-clad friends. Truth was, I built up too many barriers, denied too many of my needs during college, pulled away from my family too much, too fast, and everything backfired on me.

I started off my sophomore year with an impending sense of doom. My OCD came roaring back to life, and my days blurred together in a meaningless gray haze of depression and anxiety. I added activity after activity to my schedule, in hopes that they would quell the hopeless sadness inside and make me feel satisfied with myself and my life. It didn't work. Nothing did. For an entire semester, I allowed myself no more than four hours sleep per night, with very few exceptions, even on weekends. And it wasn't that I wasn't tired. I was. I was so tired I could hardly see straight. One day, I even fell asleep walking to class and nearly fell, face first, into a snowdrift. Even then, I didn't take a day off to rest. Rather, I handed in my paper, pried my eyelids open for one more lecture, and headed back to my room for another round of studying. I took to drinking a strange concoction of instant coffee dissolved in Diet Coke to keep myself awake, topped off with five packets of Sweet 'N Low and a generous squirt of honey.

Many eating disorder sufferers have difficulty responding to their bodily needs, and I was no exception. I came to classify my sophomore year of college as sleep anorexia, another valiant yet futile attempt to push my body to its limits. I dramatically restricted my hours of sleep in order to ensure that I hadn't taken more than I was entitled to. I had taken the saying "mind over matter" and perverted it into some sort of extremist manifesto. The problem is, of course, that the only way you can be sure that your mind has mastered your body is to kill yourself in the process. All of this proved to be a very fecund training ground for anorexia, though I didn't know that at the time.

And so my sophomore year ended. I was so drained, so emotionally and physically numb, that it took an entire summer to catch up on all of that missed sleep. Normalcy slowly returned, and memories started to fade. Even at that point, I knew that I could not keep doing this to myself. My body simply would not allow it anymore. Luckily, I wasn't going back to Hope immediately. In what was quite possibly the best decision I ever made, I had decided to spend a semester abroad studying at the University of Aberdeen in Scotland.

I loved every second of it.

This time in my life was a magical, mystical dreamland where, for the first time, I fell in with a whole group of people I could actually relate to. I met two incredibly artistic, creative women in the program, and our little trio turned Aberdeen on its head. None of us was particularly satisfied with the generic collegiate atmosphere offered at home and in Scotland, and we took very direct measures to counter that. We found open music nights at the local pubs and became friends with the extremely affable musicians who played there. Consequently, we got lessons on playing the spoons and the bodhran (an Irish drum) from a slightly intoxicated, out-of-work Scotsman. We entered a Harry Potter costume party contest and *won*, each of us getting a drink at the bar and a pound of chocolate superhero candies, which we ate all in one go. We tried our hand at British cooking, and also demonstrated down-home American cooking to our Scottish compatriots in an imitation Thanksgiving dinner that has yet to be topped. I scaled waterfalls that crashed down rocky cliffs, and trespassed in sheep fields. I earned a T-shirt by completing a Seven Deadly Sins cocktail challenge (one drink per sin). It was the best four months of my life.

Looking back, my adventures on the British Isles could have ended dramatically different than they did. My therapist is baffled that the anorexia didn't start while I was there (or during my freshman and sophomore years at Hope), since much of my disorder is tied up in fears of growing up and leaving home. And yet, as wonderful as my time in Scotland was, as much as I wouldn't change a thing, it directly precipitated my eating disorder. I didn't know it, but these would be the last happy days I would have for a long, long time. I returned after my overseas semester to the same gray world I had left behind, and I literally could not face it. My disappointment was deep and profound and, early in the spring semester of my junior year, I found myself spiraling back down into another deep depression. My time of wonderment had ended, and it was time to face reality once more.

CR

During my time in Scotland, between my late-night carousing in pubs and my experiments with British cuisine, I had managed to gain a little weight. Not much, not more than five pounds, but it was enough to make my pants just a smidgeon too tight around the waist. I began examining my reflection in the mirror, scrutinizing the slight convex surface of my stomach, the much greater curvature of my hips and butt. I felt like the gross, fat monstrosity I had always believed myself to be. I was able to forget about this monstrous me while I was overseas. Back home, I decided, rather innocently, that I needed to cut down on the fat in my diet to lose five pounds.

And that's how my anorexia began. All of the pain and suffering, the hassles and heartache, started with a simple wish to lose a mere five pounds. Only I never knew that losing weight would lead to a disease where I would lose all sense of sanity.

You can never be too thin.

Thou shall not eat without feeling guilty.

Carolyn Costin, "The Thin Commandments"

Chapter Three: Thinspirations

Hope College, Holland, Michigan, Spring 2001

For the first six months of my eating disorder, I was in complete denial of the events colluding in my life. During these months, my eating disorder hid under normal, healthy behaviors. I only wanted to lose five pounds, not destroy my life, yet this fact did not prevent anorexia from robbing me nevertheless. It's hard for me to describe this interim period of going from a small attempt at weight loss to being overtly anorexic. I first started to cut things out of my diet, a little snip here and another there. I stopped eating cheese and switched to skim milk in my coffee. Beef dropped by the wayside, and peanut butter soon followed. Individual foods soon became entire food groups, which eventually became food in its entirety. I started to exercise regularly, a routine that gradually evolved into a daily ninety-minute ritual. But that's the thing with eating disorders, and anorexia in particular—it can just sort of creep up on you. Each new rule is only slightly more constricting than the one before, so you don't really notice it. All of the sudden you find yourself living on lettuce leaves and mustard and wondering how in the hell *that* ever happened.

But it wasn't all rules and rituals at first. I enjoyed one final night of normality at a pre-spring break party, a sendoff to those lucky enough to snag tickets to the tropics. After that night, sanity was drowned in the tempest of anorexia. I wish more than anything that Sara, my roommate and best friend at Hope, had not dragged me out with her that night, that I would have stayed back in my apartment and studied. The party itself wasn't even the significant event. It was what happened the next morning, when I came face to face with what had happened the night before. From that point on, my eating disorder left the world of the hypothetical and became reality.

The bite of the Michigan winter air knocked the breath out of me as Sara and I trudged over to my friends' house, boots crunching in the fresh layer of snow on the ground. I made an attempt to mingle with other people at the party, but my attention kept coming back to the buffet of food at the center of the dining room. I couldn't keep my hands and eyes off it, constantly caressing the table, the plates and napkins, the platters of cookies. It sounds rather sad and pathetic, but I really did go to the party for the food. Having a lively crowd of my friends present at the same time was a nice bonus, certainly, but not the main reason I bundled up and dragged myself across campus. Dinner seemed like ages ago, so I decided to taste some of the goodies on the dining room table. A taste wouldn't hurt, would it? *Would* one brownie hurt? I knew that I was supposed to be keeping an eye on every scrap of food that passed between my lips, but in that brief moment of weakness, forgive me, Father, I sinned. I glanced furtively around to make sure no one was watching—if no one saw you eat it, it didn't count—then selected the smallest brownie on the chocolate mountain. I licked the warm gooey brownie off of my finger, savoring every last second of my erotic encounter with chocolate. The brownie practically melted in my mouth, and a river of chocolate ecstasy flowed down my throat as I sunk my teeth into my little forbidden treat.

I returned from the party all geared up for one last study session before vacation, assigning myself a penance for all the fun I had had. I looked down at my stomach, through my nightshirt, and saw my disgustingly gross, protruding potbelly. I shuddered as I thought of the brownie and handful of gummy worms I had consumed as I munched my way through the party. I would definitely have to make up for this tomorrow. Five hundred calories seemed like a good number—enough to keep me from losing my mind, but certainly low enough to put me in the red for the day.

Even now, several years later, I can still remember everything I ate that day after the party. I had a banana for breakfast, followed by a carton of sugar-free, fat-free raspberry yogurt for lunch. Dinner was a cup of pasta with a quarter-cup of sauce ladled over the top. Everything was safe, carefully measured and portioned out. I thought I had done pretty darn well on the first day of my new eating plan. Then Sara made pudding for dessert, the real kind you cooked on the stove, not the instant boxed stuff you whipped up in a bowl. But I just played with mine. I let it drip off my spoon and made strange designs in the vanilla puddle remaining in my bowl. I eventually said that I wasn't hungry. She seemed more surprised than hurt as she took my bowl and scraped the yellow contents down the sink. Despite hardly eating anything at all, I don't remember being hungry that day, or the next for that matter, but that is probably a testament to the power of the human mind rather than an interesting quirk of my digestive system.

From spring break until the end of the semester, I can only remember a vague montage of disconnected scenes. One evening, my roommates went out to Meijer, one of those mega-supermarkets, and bought pints of Ben and Jerry's to eat while they watched movies. I stayed in my room, studying for yet another exam, and ate a bowl of oatmeal for dinner. I recall sitting in on a chemistry exam study session at a friend's house where she served cookies during a study break. I don't remember what the exam was covering, but I cannot forget that bag of Chips Ahoy! chocolate chip cookies. I remember being horrified at finding tiny droplets of oil on the noodles from the pasta bar in the school cafeteria (why the *hell* were they cooking this stuff in oil–didn't they know how much *fat* and *grease* that added?). I meticulously, daintily, blotted the oil off with my napkin before I scooped marinara sauce onto the noodles. I created masterpieces at the salad bar: bowls heaping full of greens and veggies, sprinkled with beans, cheese, and fat-free dressing. I left everything but the lettuce and the dressing in the bowl, but see? I was eating! Nobody seemed to notice as my between meal snacks slowly dwindled to nothing.

It was no surprise when my weight began to drop. Not drastically, and not in any hideously short amount of time at first, but just steadily enough to make me fixate on food even more, and make my period start to dry up[7]. And, bit by bit, my jeans loosened. Nonetheless, I examined my shrinking silhouette in the full-length mirror on the back

---

[7] Amenorrhea, the cessation of the menses, occurs so frequently among female anorexics that it has become one of the diagnostic criteria for the disease. While many times a woman's period will only stop with drastic weight loss, amenorrhea can occur with only minimal weight loss. The regulation of the menstrual cycle is hormonal, and hormones are synthesized from fats; without enough fat in the diet, regardless of weight loss, a period can cease to flow.

of my door and saw definite room for improvement. Turning sideways, I squinted at my reflection—nope, the same flabby girl I had always seen. I closed my eyes, imagining myself having lost another ten pounds, and took a deep breath. *Yes. That's it. That's what we'll do.* Victory would surely be mine.

I was aided in my efforts by a handy little pill designed to cure me of my obsessions—Prozac. I realize this drug was not intended for use by some whacked-out anorexic-wannabe trying to make her weight drop through the basement. But that is, unfortunately, exactly what happened. The story goes something like this: once I had returned from Scotland, I quickly realized how shitty my life at Hope was in comparison and, with a large amount of prodding by Sara and various other friends, I decided to seek treatment for depression at Hope's Counseling Center. I began working with Jeanne, a woman specializing in, ironically enough, eating disorder treatment. I had no idea this would in any way be significant later on. After a number of sessions, Jeanne realized that my problems went a little deeper than your garden-variety depression and perfectionism. She suspected an underlying case of OCD, and sent me to a nurse at Holland Community Hospital to start drug therapy, where I started taking Prozac.

One of the side effects of this wonderful drug (for all the flack it gets, it *is* a rather remarkable substance) is anorexia.[8] I milked this for all it was worth. Prozac made me vaguely nauseous to boot, so on the rare occasion I *was* hungry, I typically couldn't eat anyway. Or I would force something down and it would come rushing right back up. The seafoam-green pills were a godsend. My favorite little side effect was how they acted like laxatives. For the first time ever, I finally had a flat stomach, which I celebrated by doing something completely out of character—I tucked my shirt into my jeans. Wild. Visualize a spiraling-out-of-control junior in college who is confused as hell, dabbling in an eating disorder, and half doped out of her mind on a rather potent psychotropic medication, and you have a pretty good idea of how things were shaping up as my junior year drew to a close.

What complicated matters so much in my case was that I was felled by the triple whammy of depression, OCD, *and* an eating disor-

---

[8] That is, anorexia in the medical sense of the word, meaning "a loss of appetite." Those people who have the disease anorexia nervosa are actually hungry, they just don't, for whatever reason, eat, making the moniker somewhat misleading. The most accurate term for this disease is, in my opinion, the German term Pubertatsmagersucht, a "mania for leanness." Gordon, pg. 56.

der. Now, most anorexics struggle with depression in some form or another (starving people aren't, as a general rule, happy), so that part of my story doesn't represent anything particularly unusual. But getting smacked with all three psychiatric disorders at once really knocked the wind out of me. I could handle them separately, more or less—I never said I handled them *well*—but together it was an entirely different story. When you look at it that way, it's really no wonder that I fell so far and so hard in so little time.

The especially interesting part about all of this is that depression, anxiety/OCD, and eating disorders are all associated with abnormal serotonin levels in the brain. These disorders are, of course, much more complicated than just biochemistry, although I do believe our chemical balances play a rather prominent role in determining who gets sick and who doesn't. Research is still ongoing to find out if anorexia and bulimia might also be related to abnormal levels of norepinephrine (another chemical in the brain that helps nerves send signals to one another), but the jury is still out on that one. Furthermore, both depression and OCD are very treatable with medication. Sure, not always, and not one hundred percent, but sufferers typically show a marked improvement with drug therapy. Anorexics do not. Drugs can help, but they will not by themselves alleviate any of the symptoms of an eating disorder. Popping Prozac won't keep your head out of the toilet bowl. What I believe my medication does, even today, is allow me to work on the underlying issues in therapy in a much more level-headed manner. In my eyes, I view eating disorders as a little more multifactorial than OCD or depression because I believe cultural and social factors play a larger role in the etiology of anorexia than in the other two diseases. This is why my eating disorder was able to thrive even though I was being treated with Prozac and, eventually, Anafranil, a drug commonly used to combat recalcitrant cases of OCD.

All three of my disorders came crashing down on me full-force at the end of my junior year, and I was swept away by the raging torrents. I knew how to stay afloat while battling merely depression and OCD, but the addition of anorexia had me sunk. I can still remember the exact instant in which anorexia reached out her bony hand and grabbed hold of my soul.

May 2001

After handing in the independent project I had been working on non-stop since noon the previous day, I return to the end-of-the-year task of moving my belongings out of the apartment. My parents arrive to help with the moving process. I give my mother a perfunctory hug and she gasps sharply and steps away, examining me at arm's length.

"My God, you look so thin. Look at her, Doug," my mom says. "She's just skin and bones." I give my mom a blank stare, try not to smile at the perceived compliment. I have been dieting, though at this point I think my efforts are in vain. Truth be told, I am almost ready to chuck the whole plan out the window and devour a bag of Doritos. I don't feel any thinner.

Curiosity—piqued by my mother's comments and secretly spurred on by Helga—gets the best of me and I hop on the scale the moment I returned from Hope. I mentally prepare myself for the moment I was certain would arrive, when the scale would come to rest between 130 and 135, just as it always had. Heart thudding a fierce cadence in my chest, I scrunch my eyes shut and step on the rickety bathroom scale. The dial comes to rest and I open one eye, then the other, and look down.

127.

Holy shit.

127.

I had lost weight.

Holy shit.

I do a little victory dance right there on the scale, flying sky high on a rush of adrenaline, the *hippety-hop* of my feet matching the drumroll of my pulse. I had done it. I had *lost weight*. I had really done it, my diet had finally paid off. I stifle the cry of ecstasy that threatens to escape from my throat.

The reality of what I have done hits me a moment later. If I have taken weight off, then I have to keep it off. Panic surges through me. How am I going to do that? How am I going to keep all this bloody weight off? I vow to clamp down on the rare treats I allow myself, and to up the ante on my daily runs in the pre-summer heat. The vise of anxiety around my chest loosens slightly. *It'll all be okay. Just lose five more pounds and everything will be fine.*

Liar.

Anorexia now had me as one of her sycophants and held me helpless in her thrall. My life, it seemed, would soon be sacrificed at the temple of Anorexia Nervosa. In the beginning, I had intentions of stopping once I had reached Thin Enough, wherever that destination might lie. But part of the problem is that, to anorexia, there is no such thing as Thin Enough. Helga was determined to take this thing, this plan of mine, as far as it could go. At all costs. *All* costs.

And I would pay the price.

Over.

And over.

And over.

❦

My increasingly hostile relationship with food did not go unnoticed in my house.

"Carrie?" my mom would ask in the middle of the afternoon. "Can I get you a snack or something?"

"Nope. I'm fine—still full from breakfast," I would reply, whether I was or not.

"You didn't have all that much. You really should eat something else."

"I swear to you, I'm *fine*. It's just right before my period and I'm never all that hungry right before my period."

"If you say so…" She never sounded convinced.

When I first returned from Hope, the bickering would stop there. As time progressed and it slowly dawned on my mother that my food restriction was growing more serious, her pleas for me to eat grew more urgent.

"Please eat something, just for me, *please*," she begged. "Don't you want a piece of fruit or… or… *something*? How about some strawberries? Mmmmm… you love strawberries… I bought some just for you. C'mon—just have five." Sometimes I gave in, sometimes I didn't. I got guilt pangs no matter what I did, whether I stuck to my guns, all cold and bitchy, and defiantly refused my mom's pleas, or— the perpetual weakling—I gave in and ate even a miniscule snack.

After these arguments, my mother usually asked if I wanted to call the med nurse I was seeing back at Holland Hospital and ask her about this "food thing" that was beginning to bother me.

"What 'food thing?' I don't have a 'food thing.'"

"Honey," my mom said gently, "you're not eating what you're supposed to and you know it."

"I swear to God I'm *fine*. I'm just *not hungry*. Why won't you leave me alone for *five minutes*, just five minutes? Would you *please* get off my *back*? Don't you *trust* me?" I squawked.

"Of course I trust you. It's just that… well… I really think you should call."

"Well, I'm *fine*," I huffed. "I don't need to call."

"If you're really, really sure… I'm not going to make you call if you don't want to."

I have other vague memories of the few weeks between the end of classes and my move to Atlanta. I remember having a bowl of Cheerios while my mother was getting ready for a dentist's appointment. I recall how I played with what was in my bowl while she sat next to me at the kitchen table, and then dumped it down the drain the second she left. I remember how I would intentionally stay in bed and sleep until noon so I wouldn't have to eat breakfast *and* lunch. I also remember that I saw my initial slide into anorexia not as a negative event, but as something to be celebrated, if only privately. I was completely in control of what I was eating, and it truly felt great.

As the days passed, even my dad began to sit up and take notice. One night, he had planned to take me out to dinner and then to a baseball game. By the time I learned that we were going to be eating in the stadium itself, it was too late for me to back out. Now, if we had eaten in a real restaurant, I could have ordered a salad, because every place has salads on the menu, which meant I could pick at something relatively safe. At the stadium, I would be forced to choose between an oversized fat-oozing hamburger patty and the phallic-shaped ground-up-animal-remains known as the hot dog. Why, oh why, had I opened my big mouth and agreed to go? All I wanted was a night without someone harping on me about food and eating. *Would a restaurant in a baseball stadium serve salads? They should… they must.* This failed to reassure me. The hour-long drive into downtown Detroit seemed, in my panic, to take only minutes—there was simply not enough time for me to figure out a way to squirm out of this. *I could say I'm not hungry. Would my dad go for that? What if any of this gets back to my mother? What if I have to eat a hamburger or worse, a hot dog? You can't pick at and pretend to eat a hot dog.* By the time we arrived, I had worked myself to a fever pitch. My stomach was twisted and filled with dread.

I was, however, in luck.

Not only did the little café there have salads, they also had fat-free dressing. *Thank you, God. Thank you, thank you, thank you.* I ordered a Caesar salad—hold the chicken, dressing on the side (of course)—and a Diet Coke. An anorexic's heaven. My dad stared at me, confused that I would order a Caesar salad without chicken. Later on, he offered to buy us some ice cream.

"No, thanks," I told him quickly. "But I think I may head to the ladies' room and pick up another Diet Coke on the way back. Did you want anything?"

"I thought you liked ice cream. You always used to. Don't you like sundaes anymore?" he asked, hurt that I was turning him down.

My heart broke. The little cups of chocolate malt ice cream with the wooden spoons were always my favorite part of the game and he knew this. Even though I was in college, these ice cream cups made me look forward to the seventh inning stretch like a little kid. Right there in the middle of the ballpark, I wanted to scream, *It's not you! I swear it's not! I'm sorry—I still love you. If only you could understand… I just can't eat ice cream.*

Instead, I said, "No, really, I'm not feeling all that well. Lunch just didn't agree with me and I have a headache. Go ahead and order something for yourself—don't deprive yourself on my account." He gave me that same, confused look—*what is happening to you? Why have you so suddenly changed?* But outwardly he nodded, and I headed off to the restroom, Helga triumphant at another victory. She crowed in my ear, praising me for another opportunity where I wriggled out of eating. My guilt at hurting my father's feelings was, in my mind, a small price to pay.

Events began to happen faster as the move to Atlanta approached. Days blurred together and time compressed. Each day, it seemed, I eliminated one more food from my already meager diet, or ran an extra mile. I started counting calories obsessively, adding and tallying the numbers in my head all day long. I once more returned to my five-hundred-calorie-per-day diet, generously allowing myself to consume five whole grams of fat each day—I actually thought this was sufficient—and set my weight goal at 105 pounds.

No one, not even I, realized just how rapidly entrenched I was becoming in my disorder. With Helga's help, I decided during this time that I wanted to stop dieting and start becoming an anorexic. I had assumed two things that not only conflicted, but were also flat-out wrong. First, I thought I could handle being anorexic along with living the rest of my life. Second, I didn't think I would truly be an anorexic until I weighed sixty pounds and was knocking at death's door. I never considered what I was already doing as *anorexic,* just your run of the mill weight-loss plan. Sure, it was a little, well, *drastic,* but, in my mind, I had a lot of weight to lose.

My eating disorder definitely kept me on my toes, though, especially when I went out to eat. Although I tried to squirm my way out of it any way I knew how, I was forced, more than once, to eat out in a restaurant. The ritual of anorexics at restaurants goes something like this: you arrive late because you couldn't find a pair of pants that didn't make you look like a small buffalo. You also arrive completely pissed off, because you do not want to be there, actually having to eat in front of a real, live human audience. While everyone else is laughing and joking, you become even more pissed because you, very distinctly, are not. As menus are distributed, you scan yours for anything containing the words "salad" or "vegetable." You spend ten minutes trying to order, debating between grilled chicken strips on pasta or grilled chicken strips on a bed of lettuce. You opt for the lettuce. You then interrogate the server about the contents of the sauce to determine that there is no possible way for a droplet of fat to sneak onto your plate. As you make sure he or she writes down fat-free dressing (Got that? *F-A-T F-R-E-E.* Oh, and could I have it on the side?), your requests garner strange stares from those who don't know you, and knowing sighs from those who do.

While you wait to be served, the nervous tapping of your leg (another attempt to burn off calories) accompanies the constant litany of "I-have-to-eat-oh-shit-oh-shit-I-have-to-eat." When the server sets down your plate in front of you, you first cut everything into teensy little bite-sized pieces. You then spend the next thirty minutes rearranging everything on your plate, nibbling at the lettuce, and leaving the chicken virtually untouched. You proceed to bitch about how you overdid it this time, you really indulged, and now you'll have to make up for it with another hour of cardio tonight. You then fear that everyone thinks you are a pig because you admitted that you actually ate something. They reassure you they don't. You refuse to believe them. You go home and climb the Stairmaster for forty-five minutes to work off your five bites of lettuce leaves, hating your friends for making you eat, hating yourself more for going along with it. You make a mental note to try and eat a little less next time.

These types of warped thoughts and deranged behaviors are as much a measure of an eating disorder as any objective criterion. The specialists on eating disorders get so obsessed with all of the numbers that go along with these illnesses—pulse, blood pressure, weight, number of purges per day. Not that those aren't important, but they don't always reflect the status of an eating disorder. My anorexia started when I began dieting and obsessing in January of 2001, not when my weight dwindled to 85 percent of what it should have been and kept on dropping, or when my period stopped. And my eating disorder was not cured the second I reached my target weight and my pulse picked back up again. Some of the sickest people I have met are at a perfectly normal weight, but their thoughts are detrimentally distorted. The trouble with the textbook definition of anorexia is that it doesn't always take into account the psychological processes associated with eating disorders. Anorexia, bulimia, and binge eating have more to do with thoughts and feelings than particular numbers and criteria for diagnosis.

CR

Right before I leave for Atlanta, my mom and I go see a play, and both of us immediately notice that one of the lead actresses is positively skeletal. I watch my mom's gaze flicker from her to me and back again. (I think she mentally saw me looking like that one day and knew, just *knew,* that I was going to be very, very sick by the time this ordeal was over.) "I wonder if that woman is anorexic," my mom mutters at intermission. Not being sure whether this comment is intended for my ears or not, I say nothing. "I hope that's not what you're getting," she says a little louder, turning to me.

"Mom," I say crossly, "I'm not *getting* anything. Now why don't we just sit back and enjoy the rest of the play?" I decide not to add that I rather like the jutting bones of the actress, that I secretly hope to look like her one day.

On the way home, we stop at Tim Horton's to grab something to eat. I order a coffee (hold the cream) because—surprise, surprise—I'm still full from lunch. My mom orders a bagel, asks for it buttered. The guy behind the counter slathers it on and my mother munches away as if she didn't know she was eating, like, *half a stick of butter.* "Want a bite?" She offers it to me.

I shake my head no. "I'm not hungry. Really."

"You're not hungry," my mother repeats flatly. She doesn't believe me.

"Nope. Not hungry."

"Why don't you have just a little bit of the bagel, just a quarter of it?"

I shake my head again. There is no way I will even *touch* the bagel now that it is essentially swimming in *fat.* "I'm fine," I say cheerily. My mom, stubbornly, leaves half the bagel uneaten on the dashboard, while I, just as stubbornly, ignore it. I entertain myself instead by praying that my stomach won't growl.

ɑ℞

Almost suddenly, it was time to leave Michigan for the land of mint juleps and hush puppies. My mom helped me pack some food and kitchen supplies while Helga cackled maniacally in the background. *We certainly won't be needing any of* those *now,* she chortled. I don't know what it was about the move to Atlanta that facilitated my complete mental collapse into anorexia. It could be any number of things, really. Being away from home. Living all by myself in a strange city. The fact that I stopped caring whether I lived or died, though that was likely as much a result of my anorexia as it was the cause. Regardless of the exact catalyst, the part of me that wanted to live simply went into hibernation, and all hell broke loose.

Interlude: The Life I Left Behind

CB

I pedal on the exercise bike, huffing and puffing, pushing my hair off my forehead with one hand, fiddling with the resistance thingamajig with the other. I am not paying particular attention to anyone else in the gym, burying my nose in a book instead. The door creaks open and, for some reason, I look up. There you are. I try not to gawk, though I think I fail miserably. How can you, with legs no bigger than toothpicks, stand up, let alone run yourself half to death on a treadmill, like a gerbil on cocaine? How do your arms not snap without tissue or muscle to hold them together? You, confident, cocky, don't see me ogling your pathetic silhouette. And if you do, you don't particularly care. I know.

One time, not so very long ago, I was you, the arrogant, skinny bitch determined to have her workout, she who would rail fire and brimstone at anyone who got in her way. I look at you with a peculiar mélange of longing and revulsion, finding myself horribly torn between wanting to quit recovery and become you once more, and an equally fierce desire to pull your bony ass out of this hell.

I see you. Do you know I am watching? I size you up, pass judgment on your hips and thighs, rate your thinness in comparison to mine. And, just to reassure you, I always lose that particular battle. I forget for a moment that you have a disease, just like I did, that you are heading straight toward death and there is nothing anyone can do.

You slowly disappear, waste away, cell by cell, molecule by molecule. Yet still I watch. I watch as you, so young and exuberant and vivacious, first begin your exercise regimen. I feel the sway of your limbs through the air to the beat of the music piped into your headphones. I watch those first few minutes and I, too, am convinced that you are fine and it will all be okay. I watch, however, as your energy begins to wane, and you continue onward regardless. I watch as your breathing, initially so deep and even, becomes short and staggered. Your chest seems to be gripped by a grasping, sucking *thing*, and your breath is no longer your own. I watch as time wears away this bright, promising person and turns her into a veritable exercising machine. The once beautiful human body turns dull and lifeless, all movements rendered pointless. And I watch as your knees collapse from under you and you are carried off on a stretcher, as somebody else promptly takes your spot and the whole damn cycle continues.

I see you, but I also see through you, see what others do not and perhaps cannot see. I do not see an athletic body, finely and precisely tuned; I see ropy, wiry tendons and ligaments straining to keep you from passing out. I do not see pride and strength when you complete your workout; I see the knees that buckle as you step off the treadmill and catch you at the last possible second. I do not see the tightly toned tummy, do not revel in the flat board of your abdomen; I see the secrets, the food you hid or threw up, the boxes of laxatives you stole. More than anything, I see the blue rivulets of your veins sketching your own personal portrait of pain beneath their thin coverlet of parchment skin.

You glance up at me, feeling my heavy, green-eyed gaze pressing upon your back, wondering if I can guess your dirty little secret. Oh, honey. You're not fooling anyone. Not for a minute. Eventually even the strongest safeguards crumble as this river of torment sweeps you away from shore. I do not want to watch you drown in the tempest you yourself have created, but I find myself powerless to do anything but watch. And so I sit on the sidelines and quietly observe as you starve, run yourself half to death, swallow handfuls of laxatives, barf until there's nothing left in your system and then barf once more. I watch as your once full life dwindles to merely dieting and weight loss. I scream out to God to help me find a way to save you, save your soul from the damnation of an eating disorder. But there is no answer, only silence, and I am left with a bitter dose of my own medicine.

I know it was not that long ago when someone else was the seer and I was the seen. I was that possessed girl just like you on the

Stairmaster, climbing and climbing into infinity. But now, I am the wise old sage who sadly looks on as you finish your run and complete your workout routine with stretching and sit-ups. Then, in a ritual echoed by anorexics the world over, you strip off your drenched T-shirt and soaked sweatband, your soggy socks and shoes. You take a deep breath, prepare yourself to face your fate, and step on the scale. You wiggle the little weights around to make sure that you have your precise weight, have to make sure that what you're seeing is *exactly the right number, need to have the right number.* I am haunted by how familiar these rituals are. I find I can slide them on like an old, worn pair of blue jeans if I want to. I remind myself that I have given up this life of denial and penance, of hell and heartache.

If only I knew whether to mourn or celebrate.

Whether male or female, patients who don't eat because they don't experience hunger as an appropriate desire have to be taught not only to let themselves eat but also to allow themselves to hunger.

Sandra Gilbert, in *The Obsession* by Kim Chernin

Chapter Four: The Starving Season
Atlanta, Georgia, Summer 2001

On the surface, things couldn't have looked better for me. I had secured an internship at the Centers for Disease Control and Prevention in Atlanta, working as a technician in the smallpox labs. I had found a place to live, a roommate, and had planned outings with my cousins who lived in the area. For the first time, I was thin— fashionably thin—and had a wonderful time shopping for work clothes to fit my new physique. The Prozac was starting to kick in, and I was bright and bubbly and brimming with energy. The sky seemed bluer and the grass greener than I ever remembered. I couldn't have asked for a better set of circumstances. If only I had seen the maelstrom that lurked just below the surface. No one would ever have guessed that everything would soon spiral so rapidly out of control. My mother, however, felt something through our strong mother-daughter bond, in a vague, indefinite sort of way. She had a hunch that my present euphoria was only the harbinger of something infinitely more sinister. But she was the only one who noticed.

"Are you sure you should be going to Atlanta?" she would continually ask me as I packed my belongings. "Are you *sure* you're going to be okay?"

"Of *course* I'm going to be okay. Everything will be fine. Trust me."

"Are you positive?"

"*Trust* me."

"If you say so… Promise me you're going to take care of yourself."

"Okay, okay—I *promise*."

I wasn't lying. I genuinely believed I could handle everything: being on my own, working in a fairly high-pressure environment, maintaining a strict diet and exercise regime. I saw my increasingly limited food choices and escalating exercise routine as evidence of my commitment to take care of my body, not destroy it. My hips outlined a little hula of smugness and arrogance, for everything in my life was in place.

Just listen to me, whispered a beguiling Helga. *I'll show you a Carrie you never even dreamed was possible. All you have to do is lose another ten pounds.*

Just when *did* things begin to fly out of control? The weight loss is an obvious place to start, but it's certainly not the only factor. I didn't know my OCD would rebel against the Prozac and crop up once again. I didn't know that I would get to Atlanta and freak out about being on my own in a strange city where I didn't really know anybody. I was involved in an interesting balancing act, standing precariously in the middle of a seesaw—my life could either go up or down from where I stood. Deciding to pursue weight loss at the expense of everything else tipped the balance and I fell down, down, down.

My parents and I embark on the drive to Atlanta, a thirteen-hour odyssey down Interstate 75. I remember the trip as a series of restaurants and meals. We start off the day at Dunkin' Donuts. I order a cappuccino. "I'm not really hungry first thing in the morning," I say. My parents give me a long look, then order muffins and coffee. I pretend to sip my cappuccino, wondering what lipid-laden crap they had used in this thing. Helga asks, *Okay, Carrie, what would a good anorexic do in a situation like this?* I pour half of it out at a rest stop while my mother uses the bathroom.

We stop for lunch at one of those Italian fast-food places and I order a garden salad and, for the sole benefit of my parents, a plate of spaghetti with marinara sauce. I find low-fat Italian dressing, squirt a little of it onto my lettuce, and munch on my greens like a content rabbit, all the while twirling my spaghetti noodles around on the plate. I finish the salad, but leave half the spaghetti on my plate. "I'm full," I say earnestly. To be honest with you, I was beginning to think I really was full. I wasn't falling over with hunger pains, so I figured I had to be at least somewhat filled up. For dinner, I order a spinach salad on pizza crust, eat half of the spinach, and bring the rest with me to have "once my parents had left."

And so we arrive in Atlanta. I meet up with my cousins who are in the area, go out to dinner with them, exchange phone numbers. My parents help me move my stuff into my new, swanky apartment, then head off for a mini-vacation on their own. They first make sure to point out the new ice cream shop that has just opened up next to the apartment complex. I smile and nod, thinking *fat chance*.

As I watch my parents drive away, I have terribly mixed feelings. I don't want them to go and leave me here alone. I don't know anyone here in Atlanta, sans my cousins, who live about an hour away. And we aren't exceptionally close, anyway. I think about how now it is just me—one small, scared little girl in a very large and strange city. *It's better if your parents leave… if you don't have any friends or family down here… because if you don't have anyone, then no one can make you eat.* Despite the immediate emptiness I feel, Helga's voice comforts me. Somehow staying down here by myself suddenly sounds a lot more appetizing.

So. I begin the somewhat arduous task of making myself at home. I trek over to the drugstore across the street, buy a bathroom scale, a calorie counting guide, cleaning supplies, some candles, and a box of stationery. I go grocery shopping, pick up about ten cartons of fat-free yogurt, a tub of fat-free cottage cheese, a head of lettuce, and a bag of baby carrots. I set to work organizing my closet, arranging my shirts by color. I then tackle my three shelves in the pantry, alphabetiz-ing the dry goods I brought with me and precisely arranging the cans and boxes so that the "Nutrition Facts" labels face outward. I carefully place the bathroom scale just off the main pathway from my bedroom to the bathroom, so that I will have no excuse not to step on it every time I walk past. I think of putting the scale in the pantry, below my shelves of food, so I can keep myself motivated when I grow weak, but I decide that would probably worry my new roommate.

And, no, I didn't think I was being neurotic.

The night before my first day of work, I toss and turn, panic-stricken that something will go wrong. *What if my car battery dies? What if I get a flat tire? What if I spill something on myself?* Or, worst of all, *What if I'm the fattest one there?* I run out to my car three times in my boxer shorts and flip-flops. I turn it on to make sure everything is working, turn it off, lock and unlock the doors five times, double-checking to make sure everything is fine. Then I creep back to my apartment, pee, strip off all my clothes, hop on the scale, check to make sure I haven't gained any weight in the hour or so since I last visited the scale, put my pjs back on, and crawl back into bed, where-upon the process begins all over again.

I awake for my first day of work feeling worse than the night before, when my noisy, racing thoughts had finally quieted enough for me to drop into a fitful doze. I debate, briefly, the wisdom of eating breakfast. I tell myself that my stomach is too jumpy to keep anything down and instead opt for a large travel mug of black coffee. I drive halfway across Atlanta for an intern orientation session, terrified that I will be late. I arrive forty-five minutes early. I spend the morning filling out endless forms, getting fingerprinted for security clearances, and finding out where the labs are located. We are dismissed for lunch once we receive our afternoon assignments, and, seeing as I have not talked to a single soul, I think I'm home free.

My luck doesn't hold up. Due to a mix-up, another girl and I end up getting delayed for forty-five minutes. Once everything gets sorted out, the secretary drawls, "Both of you gals from out of town? Why don't you grab some lunch together before you head back to the main campus, get to know each other some?" Shit. What am I supposed to do? I shoot a glance at the other girl, but she is smiling and nodding. I feign a smile of my own and we set off.

At McDonald's, I nibble at a grilled chicken sandwich (no mayo), and take a giant swig from my large Diet Coke. I fold up the remainder of my sandwich in the wrapper, telling the girl I'm really just too nervous to eat anything. The second I get home from work that evening, I fire up my computer and head to the McDonald's website, figuring they have to have nutrition facts in there *somewhere*. I soon discover that my sandwich had 360 calories and seven grams of fat. I panic at having exceeded my fat gram intake for the day, then reassure myself that I couldn't have had more than five grams, since I threw half of the sandwich away. I spend an hour in the fitness center, frenetically climbing on the Stairmaster just in case I *had* consumed more than those acceptable five grams.

❧

As starvation set in for real, I began to do interesting things with my food. I never sat down and thought, *Hmmm… what's the strangest thing I can possibly eat?* Instead, bit by bit, my tastes changed. I made a bowl of fluffy white rice and ate it using a celery stick I had covered in mustard, dipping it in the rice and licking it off, grain by grain. I made a sandwich out of low-cal bread and a jar full of sandwich pickles. I covered my fat-free cottage cheese with Mrs. Dash and ate it one curd at a time. I ate an entire one-pound bag of raisins in a single sitting, wholly for their laxative effect. It's hard to explain what would drive a person to eat things like this, because, regardless of what your mind thinks, your body wants to eat. Your body will fight self-imposed starvation any way it can, and it was the mastery of this primal urge that enabled my anorexia to thrive.

This phenomenon of food obsession is not limited to anorexics and modern-day dieters. As a group of conscientious objectors during World War II were exposed to a reduced-calorie diet (around seventeen-hundred calories per day, which was more than *triple* what I was consuming), their thoughts and dreams began to center around food. These otherwise perfectly healthy young men ate strange concoctions of food and beverages, very slowly, and hoarded food away for when they might "really" need it. These men likewise did something of particular importance—they binged. And then they came back to the dieticians blubbering with guilt, vowing to somehow "make up" for what they had eaten.[9]

Well, now.

Anorexics *don't* hate food. We're frightened of it, to be sure, but there's no denying that we love it. Indeed, it is precisely *because* we love it so passionately that we are terrified of food. Not that we don't try to hate it—we try valiantly—but the more we try to pretend that we only like steamed vegetables, the more we dig ourselves into a hole where the only way out is to eat and gain weight. And the longer you go without food, the more you become obsessed with it, and the more appetizing everything becomes.

As a consequence, I began to eat only foods that I could hardly stand because I was terrified to be around food that I liked. After all, if I liked a food, I might eat it and enjoy it, something Helga simply would not allow. That fear lay at the core of my eating disorder—my fear of pleasure. Having fun and enjoying myself just seemed so spineless and frivolous, and I was afraid of becoming any morally weaker than I already was. I am, and have always been, afraid to let loose and relax, to fly by the seat of my pants and just enjoy myself.

---

[9] Orig. study by A. Keys, 1950s. Cited in R. Seid,
Never Too Thin: Why Women are at War with Their Bodies

I learned, instead, to content myself with the ethereal high created by starvation. It was a phantom bliss, to be sure, but the first few weeks of my internship were almost euphoric. There were, however, a few telltale signs that everything wasn't going quite as perfectly as I had deluded myself into believing. It was during this time that I began to fast, holding a contest with myself to see how long I could go without eating. I subsisted solely on Diet Coke, black coffee, and chewing gum. My exercise routine grew rigid and harsh, demanding more and more of my dwindling energy. I would climb off the treadmill and have to sit down on the floor because my legs would no longer hold me up. I began to wear a fleece jacket around the lab because I was so cold all the time; I became impervious to the muggy Atlanta heat. Where once my diet had made me feel good, I soon began to feel miserable. Seeing the number drop on my scale would make me feel better momentarily, but the adrenaline wore off quickly and I went back to the fruitless task of lowering that number even further.

And no one in Atlanta noticed. No one knew the signs, knew that eating strange combinations of foods at strange times of day was a very potent and obvious sign of malnutrition and impending starvation. They didn't know to question my sudden need to wear sweaters and jackets over my clothes, even when the humid Atlanta air clung to everything like silk. No one, not my coworkers, not my roommate, no one, said a damn thing. I was happy about this at the time, because I knew it bought me more time to continue to self-destruct. That being said, my friends and coworkers had nothing to compare my behaviors to. I arrived in Atlanta eating like a nut, so to them it was entirely likely that I was just a little, well, *bizarre* in my eating habits.

Other habits of mine became increasingly peculiar as my OCD roared back to life with a new vengeance. The need to organize and rearrange things, over and over and over, started to plague my life. If the office supplies on my glass-topped desk *didn't look exactly right*, I would have to clear everything off and put them back in an acceptable order. After, of course, I sprayed the desk down with Windex. And I wouldn't just do this once. I would do it two, three, four, five times in a row because, *something*, I would say to myself, finger tapping against my cheek, *is out of place*.

Symmetry became more and more important, as did my systems of organization. My books had to be grouped by subject, then alphabetized by author and title. My shirts traversed the full spectrum, from red to violet. I was briefly stymied by my multi-colored shirts, until I made a separate little section for them. And I couldn't go to bed unless I had checked the deadbolt and chain on the front door five times. Four was very definitely not enough. My roommate would look over from her perch on the couch as she heard the *snicksnicksnicksnicksnick* of the lock turning in the door, and then turn back to whatever was flickering on the TV.

My obsessions, which I knew had the habit of changing on the spot, mutated once again. Not only was I fastidious about germs, but dirt and grime became Public Enemy No. 1. I scrubbed and scrubbed at the black tiles in my shower, working myself into a complete tizzy for upward of four hours because I couldn't get the streaks out. I would incessantly mop the bathroom and kitchen floors, then scrub them on my hands and knees every night to make sure I had removed every last hair and speck of lint. I would continually wipe off the countertops, and scour the sinks with Soft Scrub at least once a day. Before this, I had never worried about anything like "streaks" or stray hairs. My general housekeeping philosophy—up until then—was borrowed from one of my friends in Scotland: clean enough to be healthy, dirty enough to be happy.

I didn't want to admit that I was having an OCD relapse. I clung to my behaviors, though distressing, as my lone link to sanity. I already felt like I was only seconds away from a complete mental collapse. If I abandoned my rituals, I wasn't sure what I was going to do with myself. More than that, I think they were a wonderful red herring—they took the attention off of food, the obsession I was considerably more desperate to keep under wraps.

Then my roommate asked if I would mind dog-sitting with her for a couple of weeks. I had met the dog, a rather large bull mastiff named Moose, when I first came to town, and he seemed an amiable enough pet. I was painfully aware that a dog would throw a rather large wrench into my cleaning schedule, but I agreed because he didn't really have anywhere else to go and I was desperate for company in the evenings. I also had no idea what I was really getting into. He arrived, in all his slobbering glory, one Friday afternoon in mid-June.

It was love at first sight.

I don't know what it was about that dog—he was terrified of people (though, in terms of sheer bulk, he outweighed nearly everyone he met), soaked the carpet with his drool, and managed to leave traces of his coat everywhere he went. When I took him for a walk, he would bolt at the slightest provocation, yanking me off my feet and face-first onto the cement unless I braced myself. He once even tried to jump in the shower with me. One night, as I was scrubbing the bathroom floor, bawling and blubbering because I was fat and everything was so dirty and it wasn't fair, I heard the door creak open. I turned around and was greeted with a big wet tongue up the side of my face. I wrapped my arms around Moose, doggy breath and all, and let him lick up my tears.

From then on, my obsessions and compulsions around the apartment never had a chance. I began to laugh at the lines of drool streaking the walls as Moose galloped through the apartment. I stopped sitting on the floor for hours, searching out every last hair, and started sitting on the floor playing with the dog and his squeaky toys. After only a couple of days, I no longer banned Moose from my bedroom and bathroom, and I only scoured the sinks and toilet bowl every couple of days. Once, I even waited until bedtime to wash my dinner dishes, a task usually done immediately following my "meal." With the arrival of Moose, a huge weight had been lifted off my chest. I decided it was okay to be a little dirty.

As for my eating, well, that was another story entirely.

Although my cleaning frenzy slowly abated, my rituals surrounding eating and exercising intensified. I added half an hour of calisthenics to my hour-long exercise routine. I would climb off the Stairmaster or treadmill, terribly lightheaded, and have to hold on for dear life as the world around me tipped madly toward my face, sliding in and out of focus. I soon decided that five hundred calories per day was far in excess of what I really *needed* to eat. So I started to cut back. A snip here, another there. Soon I was eating three hundred calories a day, then only two-fifty. Some days, I didn't eat at all. It was as if I was playing a game with myself, a ridiculous little game that I had no way of winning, to see how far I could push myself before I fell.

Thing is, you never know until you fall.

☙

One of my cousins worked on the main campus of the CDC with me, and I stopped by to see her one Friday during lunch. That is, at the time when normal people ate lunch while I merely wandered the cafeteria sipping a cup of hot herbal tea. We chatted for a few minutes, and then she asked, "Why don't you come over for dinner on Sunday? We're having a barbeque and making homemade onion rings." What could I say? Sorry, I don't eat anymore? By the way, how does your toilet flush? Can it handle a good plateful of puke? I didn't want my parents to somehow learn that I was isolating myself and avoiding food-based functions. So, before I knew what was happening, I had agreed. I realized that I was going to have to do some serious fasting and exercising tonight and tomorrow to make up for it. I vowed not to eat another thing until dinner on Sunday, and to run for an hour each day.

On Sunday morning, it suddenly hit me. I was going to have to eat. Like, pick-up-a-fork-and-put-it-in-my-mouth eat. None of my nice, safe gnawing at one baby carrot per hour in precisely twenty-five bites. I thought of the oversized apple I'd nibbled at the day before, felt it lie hard and heavy in my stomach. That had to have been at least, like, 125 calories. Pig.

I arrived at their house with some flowers from the local farmers' market and the dregs of a cup of coffee I had bought for the drive over. I smelled the ribs on the barbeque out back and coughed to cover the sound of my stomach noisily protesting my hunger strike for the last few days. I sat down and played with their two dogs for a while, the smell of Moose driving them absolutely wild. After getting me a glass of water, my cousin opened a can of wet cat food. I had always thought canned pet food smelled revolting, but I had never had a whiff while I was starving. *Hmmm… that doesn't smell half bad.* I started to drool. *Don't act like Moose, you idiot.* I mentally cursed my cousin for preparing the rest of dinner in the kitchen because it meant I couldn't have a lick of the cat food. Just a lick. A little one. It wasn't "real" food—it wouldn't count. Would it? The night before, I had nibbled at one of Moose's doggy treats because, well, they smelled so good and they weren't people food so they didn't count. Right? I was horrified to find I kind of liked them.

In my stomach, the vile concoction of two cans of diet soda and two and a half pots of strong, black coffee sloshed around and I felt positively green. Maybe it was from smelling the food. Yeah, that was it—I was just too delicate to be around food any more. I went back to playing with the dogs and tried to coax the cat out from behind the couch. No luck. So I went out onto the back deck where my other cousin manned the grill. He lifted the cover and showed me the ribs he'd been barbequing all afternoon. I vaguely considered lifting my shirt to show him mine. Nausea continued to roll over me and instead, I crossed my arms over my stomach and bent forward.

"Are you okay?" My cousin came over to me. "You look pale."

"I'm fine." I gave him a false little smile, my lips absolutely white. "It's probably just the heat. I think I'll go back inside and cool off."

I made it about two feet, then bolted into their kitchen and threw up, noisily, into the sink.

"What's wrong?" my cousin's wife asked, as my coffee and cans of Diet Coke came rushing back up with a giant acidic *slosh.*

"Lunch… must not have… agreed with me." I smiled weakly, then puked again.

"Here." She gave me a mug of milk. "Drink this."

I nodded my head, took a tiny sip. I tried to get a look at the carton to see if it was skim, but by the time I looked up, the milk jug was already back in the fridge.

"Dinner's ready!" my cousin called from the back deck, and I helped him carry the barbequed ribs and deep-fried onion rings inside. There were also ears of corn on the cob, and slices of fresh watermelon for dessert. My stomach growled noisily, insistently, rendering my "I'm not that hungry" excuse useless. I picked the smallest rack of ribs and nibbled at the smallest ear of corn. I tried one of the onion rings, leaving the rest of them on my plate because "my stomach is still kind of upset." By the time we had finished dinner and were heading out to the back deck to have our watermelon, I had decided that if I was going to eat, then I may as well *eat.* Chin dripping and slurping noisily, I gobbled down what seemed like a watermelon feast—four whole wedges—spitting the seeds into the backyard.

On the way back home, I mulled over my day, my stomach full for once. And then I panicked—I was not supposed to be feeling this way. If I was hungry, everything was okay because I was losing weight. If I *wasn't* hungry, then not only would I not be losing weight, I might be gaining. The longer I considered this, the more I realized I was going to have to do something about it. I knew it was too late to try throwing up, and besides, I really wasn't all that good at it. But I knew I just *had* to get this food out of me. There had to be some way.

As I drove by the drugstore, about to pull into my apartment complex, I was struck with a brilliant idea. I immediately did a U-turn, tires squealing, and headed back to the drugstore. I walked in, extremely confident. I found the aisle that sold laxatives, and contemplated the wide range of boxes. I didn't want something too gentle because that might not get all the food out. On the other hand, I didn't want to start out with extra-strength because I didn't know how I was going to react. In the end, I bought two boxes of pink "Women's Laxatives." I took them into my bathroom, read the back of the box—"Take two as needed." I doubled it and swallowed four, figuring I could always take more if my insides didn't completely empty.

I went to bed, content that my problem had been taken care of, casually waiting for the laxatives to work their magic. In the middle of the night, I was awoken by a deep, searing pain in my gut. I curled up, hoping it would go away. It didn't. My colon felt like it was going to explode, so I staggered into the bathroom, still doubled over in pain. Rushing over to the toilet, I took the biggest dump of my life. Momentary relief. I still felt some residual muscle pain, but I headed back to bed. An hour later, I awoke again and did the exact same thing. By the time my alarm went off the next morning, the laxatives had finished their hideous work and I felt marvelously empty once again. I would later learn that laxatives don't really keep any calories from being absorbed by the body, that it's all water weight you're losing. Despite this knowledge, I kept right on taking them, because I simply loved the feeling of purity an empty digestive system brought. Though I am disgusted by the actual act of purging, the high I felt afterward, the saintliness, the freedom from everything earthly and base, kept me coming back for more.

The morning after my first night with the laxatives, as I did every morning, I examined my silhouette in the mirror, checking to see if the belly and butt were flat. Did the thighs touch? Oh, God. They did. They weren't supposed to. *Cosmo* magazine said so. Did I even read *Cosmo*? Never. Did that matter to me? Not in the slightest. I grabbed at the flesh of my thighs, gave it a jiggle. Cellulite. A lot of it. Damn. Damn damn damn. I stomped around the bathroom in a pure fury, a whirling dervish of insults racing inside my skull. Would you just *look* at this *body* of mine? *Look at it!* What in the *hell* am I *supposed* to wear? Every *scrap* of *clothing* that I *own* makes me *look* like a *bloody cow!* I can't *believe* it. I just *cannot* believe it. Worthless *lump* of *lard*. I shook my head in disgust, searching for a pair of baggy jeans that would hide my layers of blubber.

For all that I felt like a beached whale, I also knew that my clothes were getting bigger, knew precisely what that meant. I could comprehend, vaguely, that other people must see me getting thinner, because I could see the scale slip a little lower each day. I realized that by the time I arrived home, I was going to be in some serious shit for losing so much weight. My parents were going to flip when they saw me. But, before I would stop dieting, I wanted to be able to look at myself and see Thin Enough. I still couldn't. When I examined my reflection in the mirror, I saw the same person I had always seen. Thus I felt compelled to keep going.

On my phone calls home, my mother had been asking how I was eating, and I told her, "Just fine." I didn't think I was lying. I truly didn't see anything wrong with my eating habits. I knew they didn't quite qualify as "normal," but they were hardly pathological. Or so I thought. And, sure, I was losing weight, but that was kinda the point. I sure as hell didn't hope I was tormenting myself like this if my weight wasn't dropping.

That's how I saw anorexia at first, as some kind of torture. It was a torture that created a disembodied, psychedelic pleasure for me, but it was still a form of masochistic torture. As time wore on, my attitude toward starvation slowly began to shift. When I first arrived in Atlanta, I was denying myself sustenance. Food was off limits. Now I *didn't have to* eat, not if I didn't want to. And I sure as hell didn't want to. Instead of *punishing* myself by not eating, I began to *reward* myself by not eating. After a while, I began to enjoy the hunger, embracing it instead of fighting it, becoming one with it, rising above it. I saw hunger as the epitome of saintly purity and obsessive control. Soon, no matter what kind of day I had, I muddled through it by denying myself food. Eating became a question of morality, not necessity.

> We must ask ourselves if we are 'entitled' to nourishment. We have to be 'good' enough—work out enough, diet enough, and above all, be slim enough—to deserve it. We have distorted the exhortation not to overeat into the conviction that eating itself is a suspect process, that our bodies need only the barest minimum of food, and that eating more is 'bad.' We are encouraged to feel guilty if we eat the bad and enjoy it."[10]

During my time in Atlanta, my weight had plunged frightfully, from an already waif-like 125 pounds in mid-May to a skeletal 105 pounds as June drew to a close. I was at my original target weight months in advance, and I thought, hell, this is so easy, may as well keep going. Naturally, none of my pants fit anymore. They drooped down around my butt, the hem sagging and continually tripping me up. My shirts started to fall off my shoulders. What little breasts I once did have flattened against my bony sternum. As I shrank down to nothing, I found myself having to continually tighten my watch band, and took to wearing my rings on my thumbs to keep them from sliding off my fingers. Even my shoes started to rattle around on my feet.

---

[10] Seid, pg. 25.

To be honest, I loved losing weight, loved the emptiness in my insides as I simultaneously fasted and swallowed laxatives like candy. I felt ascetic. I was invincible. It was a kind of euphoria unmatched by any legal substance. There is a very real phenomenon called a starvation high, where colors seem more vivid, lights brighter, and sounds crisper. Like a drug-induced high, this feeling can leave you as suddenly as it comes, and I frequently found myself having to sit down or risk passing out. I usually managed to come up with a plausible excuse as to why I needed to sit down *right this minute*. I had, sadly, grown accustomed to the constant lying.

Everything that came out of my mouth was a lie. Every last word. They started off small, those little white lies that escape all of our lips from time to time. Some days, I would vow to tell the truth when people asked, and admit that my life wasn't all rosy, but the lies just came popping out anyway. Then they blossomed into something bigger, a demon with a life of its own.

How are you? Are you feeling okay? Did you eat breakfast (lunch, dinner, a snack)? Did you exercise? Purge?

Fine. Yes. Yes. No. No.

Lies. Lies. Lies. Lies. Lies.

I hated it.

I hated lying then, I hate it now, and I hate even more how willing I was to go along with these little schemes Helga planned. Looking back, it was as if my mind was like one of those hijacked planes on September 11—not under its own control, though it was flying, hurtling toward disaster.

CR

By the end of June, I was thoroughly entrenched in my eating disorder. I could not have stopped, even if I wanted to. And I soon found I wanted to. Even if it was for just a meal or two.

Everyone in the lab had decided to order pizza for lunch one day while I was closeted in a back room finishing up some tests. One of the other technicians poked her head in the room. "Should I order some slices for you? We're getting deep-dish…" she said, trying to tantalize me. I stared at her, horrified. How was I going to get out of this one? My heart started to pound. I took a deep breath. "I don't like pizza."

"You don't like pizza?" she asked, incredulous. "How can you not like pizza?"

"I just... don't. That's all."

"Is that the reason you gave me that panicked look when I asked you if you wanted any?"

"Yeah... that's it." I shrugged and nodded my head. "Besides, I brought a lunch, and I really need to eat up that lettuce before it goes bad." She gave me a look, surely wondering how I could prefer a plain salad to pizza, but she thankfully didn't bother me about it any further. As she walked out the door, though, it hit me—I *wanted* pizza. Badly. Like, really *really* badly. And this wanting scared the shit out of me. I could see myself chasing her down the hall, yelling, "Wait! Order enough for me, too!" But the words stuck in my throat and I stayed silent. Later, they offered me leftovers, which I again found myself declining. I did not do this consciously. I very simply, very automatically, said, "No thanks, I'm full," or some variation thereof. I thoughtfully munched on my little rabbit lunch and realized I had convinced myself that I actually preferred salads to pizza. I realized, intrinsically, that there was something wrong with this.

There were two parts of this particular episode that spurred me to seek help. One was the sheer panic with which I faced eating even a single slice of pizza. Here I am, working with smallpox, arguably one of the most lethal viruses known to man, not even batting an eyelash, yet I couldn't face a simple slice of pizza. I knew, in some primal way, that this was not normal. The fact that I wanted the pizza and I *couldn't have it,* no matter how much I might have desired it, also struck me. I was perplexed—how could I want something and literally forbid myself from having it? Because of these two realizations, I could no longer deny that something was wrong. If only I could figure out how to help myself...

I remember broaching the subject with my parents sometime at the end of June. I never said, "I think I have an eating disorder," in so many words, I just nonchalantly wondered if it might be okay if I went to see a therapist. My parents had been aware of my OCD flare-ups, and I implied that the problem had as much to do with my cleaning obsessions as any eating problem. I didn't want them to worry about me, so I downplayed everything. "Besides," I said, "I don't really know anyone down here, and it would probably do me good to have someone to talk to."

My problem was that I wanted it both ways—I wanted all the perks of anorexia and none of the negative consequences. I didn't want to stop losing weight, but I also didn't want to feel like a wrung-out dishrag at the end of each day. I was perfectly willing to seek help for whatever it was that was bothering me, as long as no one asked me to make any changes to my lifestyle. When I started therapy, I deluded myself into believing that I could continue to starve myself as the rest of my life magically improved.

I clearly remember being unable to sleep the night before my first appointment with the therapist, though I'm still not sure whether from starvation or nerves. I know I was distinctly nervous about how I would tell people at work I was seeing a therapist for an eating disorder. I initially decided to keep my mouth shut, but as time passed, I grudgingly acknowledged that someone would have to know since Anne (my therapist) didn't have any Saturday appointments. So I went in to talk to my immediate supervisor in the lab. I stared at my feet, uncomfortable, not knowing what to say. I mentally shrugged my shoulders and thought, hell, it couldn't be *that* bad. Could it? "Umm... I don't know if you were aware, but, um, well... ithinkihaveaneatingdisorder." I blinked and looked up at my supervisor. "So would it be okay if we could, um, work out some system where, um, I could meet with a, um, therapist and, um, come in early for, um, work?" I was certain a lowly summer intern didn't merit such special treatment.

"I noticed you were on the skinny side, but..." She looked at me wistfully as I glowed at the compliment. "I wish I could say I had your problem." Why did everyone say this? I was cursed with the amazing capability of self-destruction and mutilation, and you wanted to be just like me? How crazy was that? What did this say about our society and these so-called "problems"? Worse yet, what did this say about those who wished a psycho-physical disorder upon themselves, all in the name of being thin?

"No, you don't," I reassured her hurriedly. "Believe me, no, you don't."

"Well, I noticed you didn't eat a whole lot, but I thought that was only because I ate so much." I briefly debated telling her that the lettuce leaves and few licks of aspartame-laced yogurt was pretty much *all* I ate, that I would run and run and run until my legs gave out, and then I would force myself to run some more and follow this with sit-ups and leg lifts. I decided, however, I'd had enough honesty for the day and bit my tongue. "But don't you worry about a thing, dear." She reached out and patted my shoulder, her hand resting for a moment on the bony elbow that jutted out of the long line of my arm. "Your health is most important. We'll take care of everything."

One of my co workers, Linda, was less surprised when she learned I was an anorexic. We met for coffee one day—I remember because I was extravagant and indulged in a small nonfat café mocha—and she just kind of nodded when I told her. "I kinda figured something was up," she confided in me. I asked her what had made her think I had an eating disorder, what gave me away. "I just walked in one morning and saw this really, really skinny girl in really, really baggy pants, and I knew. I just knew."

"That's fair enough," I answered quietly.

On the whole, everyone at work was very supportive of me. Outside of Linda and my supervisor, I didn't directly tell anyone what was going on, but soon others figured out what was up. Linda went out of her way to drag me down to the cafeteria every day and talk me into at least ordering a salad. I would dutifully eat a plateful of lettuce drizzled in vinegar, because at this point, even fat-free salad dressing had too many calories. Most of the time I couldn't even finish it because the vinegar was so acidic it turned my stomach. After lunch, I would soundly berate myself for being so weak. What kind of anorexic was I, anyway?

And so I headed out of the lab twice a week and showed up on Anne's doorstep. I didn't exactly give her a whole lot to work with, but I loved therapy. Especially at first. It was a fifty-minute session where I could talk all about me and *someone had to sit there and listen.* I got along great with Anne, and even started to open up to her. I suppose I figured that once I left Atlanta, I would never see her again, so what did it matter anyway? I told her about the OCD, the depression, the pizza, Moose, you name it. She loved coffee like I did, always carrying a latté with whipped cream to our early morning sessions. Once she accidentally gave herself a whipped cream moustache, which I found particularly hilarious. Best of all, she didn't insist on weighing me.

Things were going great. My weight was still plummeting, I had somebody to talk to, *and* my parents were rather willingly footing the bill. And then, one day in early July, Anne noticed my continuing weight loss.

"Have you ever considered going to a treatment center?" she asked me.

Actually, no, I hadn't. I told her this. "What makes you think I need to go to a hospital?"

"I just saw you walk through the door, with all your layers of clothing and your baggy jeans, and I realized how *thin* you had gotten." I couldn't wipe the grin off my face. Finally someone was noticing.

She continued, "Maybe you should get checked out by a doctor, to see how you're doing physically." I agreed—what on earth could possibly be wrong with me? I was certain that I would pass any test with flying colors. She finished our session by telling me, "I really do think you should look into an inpatient program."

I contemplated this therapy session as I ran laps around the Kansas-sized parking lot next to my apartment building. I thought to myself, space in a hospital should be reserved for those who *really* need it, not for some pissed-off chick playing at an eating disorder. I still didn't think of myself as sick, let alone dying. After all, I had only lost a little more than one-quarter of my body weight... and then it hit me. *If losing one-quarter of your body weight in three months* isn't *a problem, would you* please *tell me what is?*

I decided, at that precise moment, to enter the hospital. This didn't, however, keep me from pounding the pavement, my heart beating a steady *thrum-thrum-thrum* accompaniment to the scrape of my shoes against the concrete.

Even though I had decided to go into treatment, I was in denial of what "getting better" would actually involve. Again, I wanted to get well, but I didn't want to let go of my starvation rituals and stop losing weight. It never occurred to me that I would have to gain weight— serious weight—when I entered the hospital.

Then my mom dropped a bombshell—she told me one evening that, as a surprise birthday present, she was going to fly down and spend a weekend with me in Atlanta in mid-July. I didn't want her to see me, knowing instinctively that my severe weight loss would alarm her. I hadn't quite let on how many pounds I had lost, and I knew that coming face to face with her emaciated daughter would scare the hell out of her. I was also terrified of the fact that I was going to have to eat birthday cake if I stayed in Atlanta.

So, with my twenty-first birthday looming just around the corner, I casually mentioned to my parents that these "eating issues" of mine might just be a little larger than I first thought. At first, they said nothing. Then, "Well, what do you think we should do?"

"Anne suggested a place in Wisconsin—Rogers Memorial Hospital. They have a special inpatient program for eating disorders, a new one that's just starting up. I gave them a call. They're going to start an insurance assessment on Monday."

My parents had no idea what to make of all this. Neither of them had any sort of experience with even minor psychiatric problems, not to mention serious ones. "It all just happened so fast," my mom said.

"I should have just brought you home and taken the time to find the right hospital for you. Maybe if we weren't so hasty…maybe things would have turned out differently. Maybe you wouldn't have gotten quite as sick." And she was right—it *did* happen fast, and hard. Had Anne not intervened when she did, it's entirely likely I would have keeled over in cardiac arrest before I made it back to Detroit.

My parents and I were under the impression that, once I entered treatment, I would be "fixed," and the problem would miraculously go away upon discharge. Many people wrongly assume, as we did, that an eating disorder is little more than a diet that just went a bit too far. Anorexia nervosa, the complete, full-blown, let's-starve-ourselves-and-get-uber-thin-no-matter-what business, is quite a bit more complex than Weight Watchers gone awry. Society has this notion that eating disorders are just a "dieting disease," or a passing fad for a bunch of spoiled little rich brats who don't want to grow up. And it's true, from the outside it does look as if anorexics have made the autonomous decision to eat less and exercise more, to swipe boxes of laxatives off store shelves, and to shove our fingers down our throats in order to rid ourselves of dinner. The more I live with it, however, the more I am coming to see that an eating disorder is much more complex and multi-dimensional than most other illnesses—and that's what it is. A disease. One of the biggest hurdles to jump in my recovery was not wanting to relinquish control of my disorder to my treatment team. I saw anorexia as my choice, my personal little crusade, and I did not want someone, however well-intentioned, to take it from me. But the clincher is this— it was never really mine to lose.

This is not to say that I didn't have the medical profession convinced I wasn't *that* sick. Following Anne's request, I went to an acute care clinic to have a routine physical to take care of the bloodwork that Rogers needed before they would admit me. I expected someone to plunk me down on a scale, prick me with a few needles, and send me on my way. The doctor asked me why I needed the tests done, and I told him point-blank that I was about to be admitted to an inpatient eating disorder program. "Hmmm," he said. "Do you throw up? I've heard a lot of you guys do that."

"No." I was mildly offended that he referred to the eating disordered population as "you guys." He never asked about diet pills, diuretics, or, in my case, laxatives.

"When was your last period?"

"I don't know…this past May."

"Are you sure you're not pregnant?"

"I'm sure."

"How do you know?"

"Because I haven't had sex in the meantime... or at all for that matter." I didn't tell him that between the starvation and the Prozac, I had the sex drive of an ossified tree stump.

"A girl like you, a virgin? How old are you, anyway?" He turned to the nurse. "I didn't know they made virgins this old." She shook her head. "I didn't either." My dearth of boyfriends was already a touchy subject for me, and this exchange left me feeling like the biggest loser ever to walk the face of the planet.

"I didn't come here to discuss my sex life, or my lack thereof," I hissed. "I just want some bloodwork done so I can get out of here." The doctor then left the room and allowed for a one-on-one assessment with the nurse. She started out with the usual—height, weight, how long have you been experiencing these symptoms, etc. Then she asked, "Aren't you a little old to be having problems like this?"

"What do you mean by 'too old'?" I asked suspiciously.

"Usually anorexics are a lot younger... I thought you would have grown out of this phase by now."

I stared at her, astounded that someone in the medical profession could be this tactless. I racked my brain for a fitting retort, but couldn't come up with anything nasty enough, so I kept my mouth shut.

"And what about your clothing? I thought all of you wore layers and layers of clothing. You're only in jeans and a T-shirt."

"In case you hadn't noticed, it's the middle of July and about ninety-five degrees outside right now, not counting humidity. I should be burning up in jeans, yet I'm right now thinking that the Atlanta heat everyone talks about is rather overrated."

"Maybe you have a thyroid problem... that would explain the weight loss..."

My attitude, already rather sour, took a rapid turn for the worse. "Whatever... I don't really give a rat's ass what you think. Just draw my blood and let's be done with this." I couldn't believe I was going to be expected to pay for the services rendered. I returned two days later for my test results, whereupon I was diagnosed with a thyroid abnormality.

"You're not anorexic," the doctor told me. "You just have a problem with your thyroid. Do you want me to write you a prescription for a drug to help you regulate your appetite better and gain some weight?"

"I'd rather jump in front of a train." I snatched the paper printouts of my (grossly abnormal) EKG and blood tests, signed a check, and stomped out of there. Good riddance.

I returned to my apartment, whereupon I immediately raided the refrigerator. The urge to binge had overwhelmed me. Part of this urge, I would later learn, is primal and biological, driven by a body in starvation mode. The other part was pure emotion, the tidal wave of anger and frustration at this dipshit doc and his floozy nurse. It had taken all of my courage to walk into a strange place and actually admit I had an eating disorder, only to be ridiculed and dismissed. To them, my sex life was a joke fest. What was I supposed say—no men, but you should see me with a vibrator? My insurmountable frustration from all this had me lassoed to the fridge. Having attempted to purge several times already that summer, using various implements to no avail, I knew I couldn't actually swallow any food. Then I remembered a technique of chewing and spitting out food that I had accidentally discovered one day when my roommate decided to play Betty Crocker.

With this clever trick in hand, I was off and running. I first demolished the shoebox full of candy that I had been hoarding, stuffing my face with dozens of candy bars, stale Mike and Ikes, and a large bag of Reese's Peanut Butter Cups. I then made a vegan stir-fry over rice, and took it back to my room. I started shoveling bites into my mouth, spilling rice all over my bathroom floor. I then licked it up off the floor. *Food… hurry… need more food.* I rummaged through my pantry like a demon possessed, consuming an entire package of dinner rolls slathered in a can of baked beans, a sleeve of bagels, my roommate's homemade chocolate chip cookies, a box of vanilla wafers, and a half-eaten bag of M&Ms. I paused and looked around, chest heaving with exertion. My shelves, already rather spartan, were now essentially bare. I decided to run over to Kroger, intending to get just enough food for my lunches for the rest of the week. Instead, I bought a dozen Krispy Kreme doughnuts, several king-size Snickers bars, a one-pound bag of Twizzlers, and a bag of sour cream and onion potato chips, along with my usual fat-free cottage cheese and head of lettuce. I dashed back to my bathroom, where I proceeded to shove everything in my mouth. I couldn't get it in fast enough.

When I looked up at the clock, four hours had elapsed since I made it home from the doctor's office, and yet my only memory was of the wrappers that littered my bathroom floor. All the food was gone. I slumped to the floor with exhaustion. I washed my food-spattered face, cleaned the detritus off my floor, scrubbed out the nasty, food-stained toilet bowl, and collapsed into bed.

It wasn't until morning, when I took out the garbage and saw all of those crinkly wrappers and the half-chewed junk food, that it slowly began to dawn on me exactly how much food I had chewed and spit out. Horror took hold. Not only at what I had done, but over the fact that I had every intention of repeating it the second I got home from work that day.

In my heart, I knew what this was—a binge. I tried to deny it then, and I still don't like to think of it as such now—I never lost control, not me. After all, I didn't really *eat* anything, did I? *Did* I? Yet it was as much of a binge as if I had swallowed the food and threw it up later. Bingeing scared the hell out of me. I didn't know back then that one sure way to avoid these episodes of uncontrolled eating was by following a normal, healthy meal plan. So I would continue to be terrified, spending every waking moment plagued by the thought that in only a couple of seconds, I could once more be madly shoveling food into my mouth.

This fear, combined with the knowledge that I would soon be heading into the hospital, fueled a renewed desire to starve myself. This was it, my last hurrah, the last chance I would have to prove to everyone how good I was at being anorexic. So I stopped eating. Entirely. I completely panicked when my coworkers offered to take me out to a farewell lunch on my last day. What the hell were they thinking, taking a visibly eating disordered person out to *lunch*? The idea was almost ludicrous. On the one hand, I could hardly turn them down, but neither could I just go and chow down. I was, after all, leaving my job because of anorexia. I had to provide *some* sort of evidence that my eating habits were warped enough to warrant a trip to the hospital. So, on my last day in Atlanta, I ordered a plate of chicken and stir-fry vegetables at some random Thai restaurant and absently picked at my lunch. I was disgusted and terrified to find that I finished it. I shrugged my shoulders and consequently finished off a box of laxatives in the ladies' room at the restaurant. I later exchanged gifts with everyone in the lab, then headed back to my apartment to start packing.

I have always hated packing, but I especially hated it in this particular instance. I didn't know exactly where I was going, who I was going to be around, or what size my butt was going to be at the end of it. The thought of it, of going to a hospital in Wisconsin, nearly unseated me. I whirled around the apartment in a breathless daze, my roommate blessedly gone for the week, wondering if my frenetic movements were enough to burn off the calories in the small nonfat latté I had skittishly sipped for dinner. I packed my bags in a frantic hurry, not really worrying about what I was packing, so much as about cleaning out the toilet bowl of all the food I had spat in it over the past few days.

As the airplane took off from the Atlanta runway, I stared out the window, watching the lush Georgia landscape disappear under me. This was not happening. Dear God, it was not. Maybe this was all just a bad dream. A very bad dream. I closed my eyes and prayed with an earnestness unmatched since the Spanish Inquisition. I promised to eat supper if only I didn't have to leave my apartment and my job and Moose. The clink of the beverage tray snapped my eyes open, and I was handed a little packet of peanuts and a neat square napkin. I examined the cellophane for the nutrition facts on the label. Nothing. Nada. Zip zilch zero. Well, shit. *Now* what was I going to do? I caught a glimpse of a phone number consumers could call if they had questions about the nutritional value of this product. What good is *this* going to do me, way up here in the air? I stole a sideways glance at the little Japanese businessman in the seat next to me, contentedly munching away.

"You want these?" I offered the bag of miniature fatballs. "I don't like nuts." He gracefully accepted his unexpected windfall. "I get you drink?" he asked.

I mumbled another fervent prayer, this time that the man wasn't a total pervert. I nodded my head yes. "Sooooooooooooo-da," I mouthed, exaggeratedly. He bobbed his head up and down. "Coke," he said proudly, a grin splitting his face from ear to ear.

"No, no, no. Diet Coke. *Diiii-et.*" He gave me a blank look. All right, different tactic. "Water," I said, making a drinking gesture. "Water," he parroted back to me. Great. Now we were on to something here. We made the exchange, and I settled back into my seat, trying to focus on a book. The rest of the flight passed uneventfully, and before long we had touched down in Chicago.

My friend Sara met me at the airport, gave me an awkward hug hello, and helped me lug my suitcases up and down numerous stairs and escalators. On our somewhat circuitous journey to Union Station, I became profoundly aware of the fact that I could bolt and no one could stop me. I could go home. I could go back to Atlanta. I could go anywhere, really, anywhere except to some nuthouse in a hick town in eastern Wisconsin.

Sara tried to entice me into buying something from a vending machine. I stared at the selections, completely dumbfounded by the variety of products offered. My brain literally went into overload, all of my neurons flooded with the sight of FOOD. And not just any food. YUMMY FOOD. I couldn't choose. I told her that I would get something on the train, that I would find something for dinner later. She nodded, though we both knew I wasn't going to eat anything that day.

After a hug farewell, I boarded the Amtrak alone and idly watched the northern Chicago suburbs fade into southern Wisconsin farmland. The concession carts clinked by, and I decided I had been through enough trauma to warrant something besides the bottle of warm tap water in my backpack. Sipping on my diet soda, I savored my last few hours of freedom along with the aspartame aftertaste. The handful of laxatives I had taken the day before had not yet left my system and I curled up in my seat, hugging my knobby knees to my chest, while they did their dirty work, eventually unfolding myself long enough to make a frantic dash to the bathroom. I was greeted at the Milwaukee train station by a driver from Rogers Memorial Hospital, who kindly watched my bags while I made one last desperate trip to the ladies' room, this time to swallow the last of the laxatives I hadn't yet stashed away in my suitcase.

The drive to Rogers passed in a blur. The driver pointed out various Milwaukee landmarks. I was worried, primarily, that we would arrive there in time for dinner. I glanced at the speedometer. *Slow down,* I mentally hissed. *You're going way the hell too fast.* The little old man was doing fifty-five in a sixty-five mph speed limit. We were a traffic hazard as it was, but I didn't care. As the minivan pulled onto a dirt drive, I got my first glimpse of my home for the next two weeks. And it looked precisely like that—a home, replete with a front porch and shuttered windows. Only here, the glass was shatterproof. I tentatively poked my head inside the door, glanced around at the magazines scattered on the coffee tables in the front lobby. *Better Homes and Gardens* and Martha Stewart *Living.* Ooooh, goody! What could we do with these—spend an evening decorating the psych ward? French country blue would go just *fabulously* with the paper gowns they weighed us in each morning. And I think the bathrooms should be painted a woman's laxative pink. Oh, wait. They already looked like someone had puked Pepto-Bismol all over the walls.

I scrawled my name on a dozen or so forms, confirming that I, Carrie Arnold, was here of my own accord and willing to receive treatment. I agreed to allow staff to search my belongings and promised to obey all the rules of the hospital (of which, I would later learn, there were far more than I bargained for, though far fewer than I actually needed). Someone took my luggage, I didn't pay attention who, and I was escorted to the elevator by the hospital secretary. My gaze flickered between her and the door to the outside. I could make a run for it. I really could. Give the secretary a little shove and take off running. How simple. I debated this for a minute. Where would I go? I was in the middle of Wisconsin, for the love of God. Cheese country. The elevator dinged its arrival. "This way, dear." The secretary led me onto the elevator, pressed a button, and the door slid closed. My stomach sank in chagrin. Too late. Too damn late. I was led off the elevator, and the door to the unit was unlocked. My eyes darted around frantically as I was taken inside. No way out.

The door clicked shut behind me. I was locked in the loony bin.

I'm not crazy, I'm just a little unwell.

Matchbox 20

Chapter Five: Bedlam
Rogers Memorial Hospital, Oconomowoc, Wisconsin, July 2001

Some of the most sane people I have ever met spent time on psych wards. Crazy people aren't crazy because they see events differently than everyone else; they're crazy because they recognize what's really going on and can't gloss over it. A study of depressed people found that they actually perceive reality more accurately than those not suffering from depression. Fascinating.

As much as they try to boast of their differences, eating disorder treatment centers are remarkably uniform. Upon your arrival, staff[11] will search your belongings and remove anything with which you might be able to hurt yourself. This list includes, but is not limited to razors, knives, shoelaces, glass, bottles of makeup, mirrors, drawstrings, hangers, needles, scissors, nail clippers, nail files, headphones, CD players, necklaces, belts, teabags, wire-bound journals and calendars, and my stuffed moose, Casey (she had a battery-operated sound box in her paw). After staff rummages through each and every pocket, you will sort through your heap of stuff, make an attempt to neatly fold everything, get halfway done, realize that no one here gives a shit about

---

[11] "Staff" refers to any number of people who typically work on an inpatient unit, such as nurses, nurse assistants, social workers, technicians, etc. They all tend to blend together into one massive unit, save a few notable exceptions, as I soon discovered.

wrinkles, and stuff the rest into a random drawer. You will be given a folder containing a pamphlet entitled "Your Mental Health Rights," which lists what the hospital is and is not allowed by law to do, which you will pretend to read while staff finishes ransacking your luggage. The staff member who gives you the folder tells you to make yourself right at home, though neglects to mention how, considering you find yourself faced with an expanse of plastic-coated couches and polypropylene chairs. Everybody will do their best to welcome you to the floor, though you will ignore all of them because you are trying very hard to pretend that you are the only person left on the face of the planet. Someone will ask you if you want anything to eat. You will refuse because you realize you have to show everyone how a proper anorexic behaves, and eating is definitely *not* a part of the role.

"Could I get a can of Diet Coke or something?" I asked, as staff took orders for evening snacktime.

"No, but we can send up for some regular Coke," a nurse replied.

Regular Coke? Me, drink regular Coke? I don't think so. I shook my head. "No, thanks."

"Are you *sure* you don't want anything else?"

"Nope." The head nurse *tsk*ed softly, scribbled something on my chart. I was, after all, no longer a person. I was a patient.

The eerie transition from the harshness of real life to the soft and padded reality of a treatment center occurs within the first twenty-four hours. Almost instantly, I forgot the myriad issues that had brought me to this place, the mess I had made of my life. Instead, I roamed the long corridors in a daze, trying in vain to remind myself why exactly I was here in the first place. This couldn't be my life. I couldn't have left a *totally awesome* internship at the CDC, the Holy Grail of infectious disease institutes, for Podunk, Wisconsin. Actually, it was worse—the name of the town was Oconomowoc. At least you could pronounce Podunk.

A psych unit, on the whole, is like an island unto itself, and I became an island within that. About a week into my stay, I flipped through the sale flyers and noted absently which jeans were on sale and which shoes had been discounted. The ads reminded me, very profoundly, how far away my former life was. It was like I had taken up residence in another world. I could not go out to the stores that carried these items. I could not go to the mall that had the stores that carried these items. I could not get into a car to get to the mall that had the stores that carried these items. My former world was officially lost to me.

The first person I saw once I arrived at Rogers was the other anorexic woman on my floor. I almost bolted. Amy was, quite literally, the thinnest person I had ever seen, and ever hope to see. Skin and bones overqualified what she looked like. When I eventually left Rogers, I gave her a hug good-bye, and my arms gently encircled her emaciated frame. I was honestly afraid I might break her in two. Her initial appearance, in and of itself, didn't cause me to panic. But I was no longer the best anorexic I knew, and being unseated really unsettled me. I thought surely this woman must scoff at my wasted ninety-five-pound frame, plump in comparison to hers. Fat pigs like Carrie don't belong in this hospital, she must have thought. I later learned that Amy envied me, thought me lucky to have the presence of mind to get out of this stinking hell, rather than wallow in starvation as she was doing.

As pathetic and dire as her situation was, I found myself jealous of her, envying her determination and drive. Though we simultaneously pitied them, we all secretly admired those anorexics who had devoted their entire lives to self-starvation. Here was someone who had really figured out this whole eating disorder thing. Here was a woman who knew *exactly* what she was doing.

I learned later that Amy had been enduring the torments of severe anorexia since she was seventeen. By the time I met her at Rogers, fifteen years had passed, and her life was still on hold. Amy looked much younger than her thirty-two years, a fact belied by her gaunt silhouette. The moral of Amy's story wasn't how sick she was (and she certainly was sick), but rather her experience, which spoke of the futility of anorexia nervosa. If there was anything to be gained from starving oneself, I have full confidence that she would have found it. Amy had spent fifteen years in the hell of anorexia and had nothing to show for it but a wasted body and a broken heart. And, in the end, anorexia left me no better off.

CR

During the first few days, I entertained myself by playing a very interesting game in my head, much like those logic questions on standardized tests. If Mary is skinnier than Tammie but fatter than Julie, which anorexic on the unit is the thinnest? If Pammy runs three miles fives times per day and Betty bikes twenty-three miles per day, who burns the most calories? And so on, in an endless number of permutations and systems of rank. The best part of it was, each day brought on a new game, with new people and new sets of rules. My precise location within this lineup determined my mood for the entire day. Even though everyone would practically gush about how skinny I was, I was convinced that I was at the "fat" end of my little ordinal system, and nothing could convince me otherwise.

Since most of the other women in the eating disorder program at the time suffered from bulimia, I was left in a rather interesting position. I found myself the envy of everyone on the floor. Anorexia has a sort of holiness to it, the sanctity of self-denial, and the skeletal figures appear almost superhuman. Here were people that didn't have to eat, who could overcome their bodily urges. Bulimia, though it, too, despises and abuses the body like anorexia, does not deny the flesh with the same violence and passion as self-starvation. It's viewed in the psychiatric world as anorexia's ugly stepsister, and considered not as dangerous but definitely more disgusting. That both diseases can and do kill does not occur to those of us entrenched in these disorders. I wasn't quite sure how to respond to this admiration of my disorder. Part of me preened under all of the attention, the other part shied away from any extra interest my disease caused. Nonetheless, I wore my thinness as a badge of honor.

Before I entered the hospital, I was under the impression that because I did still eat, most of the time, I didn't quite qualify as a true anorexic, which is a load of malarkey, of course, but it's a common misconception, especially among those not familiar with eating disorders. Anorexia is a mind-set, a very pathological one, and it has more to do with a pattern of thinking than a particular weight or a particular limit on the number of calories consumed.

Tale-swapping in an eating disorder center occupies a large chunk of the time not spent in groups or eating (or being watched *after* eating or worrying about eating or…), and we patients cheerfully traded weight-loss secrets and methods of purging. Some were obvious, some less so. I learned which brand of laxatives worked fastest, which foods were easiest to regurgitate. I was asked how I managed to eat so little and not binge. I always shrugged my shoulders. "You got me," I'd reply. I could only talk about eating nothing but lettuce and Diet Coke—yum, yum! It made for rather boring storytelling, and so I contributed relatively little to these conversations, other than the occasional, "No, actually, I don't miss doughnuts." Which, as you might guess, was a bold-faced lie.

As much as I knew that anorexia was the more revered disease of the two, I resented that I never figured out how to purge with any sort of ease. More than that, I thought (wrongly, as it turns out) that purging freed a person from the constant worry of what to eat because you could always do something about it later. What I also didn't realize was the extra slavish worship of the porcelain goddess, the endless debate about whether to keep food down or throw it up.

"I named my eating disorder 'Kohler' because that's what I stare at on the toilet as I purge," said one of the women on the unit. "I want to flush him away along with my food," she recounted mournfully. Did that matter to me? Of course not. I too wanted to be able to shove my head down the toilet and rid myself of the terrible burden of having to live with every bite I ate. I quizzed the other women there about methods of throwing up, discovering all sorts of utensils that aided the process of gagging oneself. All in all, I came to possess a remarkable library of knowledge on vomiting, the contents of which I would not put to use for many more months.

The doors came out of nowhere. They always did, every last time. As the summer progressed and my condition worsened, even though I was hospitalized, I developed the bad habit of running into walls and doors. My vision would dim, and before I knew it, a wall or door would be there, right in front of me, and I couldn't change my stride in time to avoid it. During my time at Rogers, I was on a crash course with the walls several times per day. Each time I stood up, the ground would tip madly, gaily, up at me, and blackness encroached as my vision narrowed down to nothing. I, being a stubborn little brat, refused to admit that my eyesight was in any way compromised by my current poor medical condition, and would keep on walking even as my panorama was essentially nil.

"You okay there?" The social worker who admitted me gently pulled at my elbow as I rebounded off yet another door. I grinned sheepishly. "Must have stood up too fast," I mumbled. She nodded, knowing full well the real reason why I mistook the door for the door*way*. By that time, however, I was used to my blood pressure bottoming out every time I changed positions, and had long since accustomed myself to allowing my vision to clear. I soon got a good feel for the layout of the unit, and managed, for the most part, to stagger down the center of the hallways and avoid all of those pesky doors.

And so I came to make myself at home in the hospital.

CR

Rogers Memorial Hospital has an interesting approach toward eating and meal plans. They don't actually try to force patients to eat, realizing that somebody doing it on his or her own accord is much more powerful. And it is, of course, but considering that we wouldn't *be* in a mental institution if we *could* eat on our own, this philosophy is somewhat flawed. At the time, however, I loved this policy because I didn't actually have to eat anything, though I realize now it was stupid and naïve to continue to starve myself in the hospital. I would be remiss to blame them for my actions, yet my inpatient treatment at Rogers was almost entirely in vain. I restricted my food intake to virtually nothing for the two-week duration of my stay.

I can say this for Rogers—they did have a firm policy about locked bathrooms, which we all needed, regardless of our varied histories with purging. Though we begged and pleaded to have them opened, the doors remained locked, making this the one rule I was pigeonholed into obeying. What was worse, staff was required to listen to you talk while you tinkled, to make sure you didn't simultaneously barf up your food. These conversations were stilted; no one quite knew what to say. We were trying to play normal in a situation that had become profoundly abnormal, and it started to wear thin after a while. After a few days, we managed to convince staff to leave the bathroom doors unlocked in the middle of the night so that we didn't have to have the midnight (male) nurse come chat with us while we peed. I never abused this privilege, and I'm fairly certain everyone else managed to behave themselves, too.

I don't entirely blame the hospital for the miserable outcome of this two-week stay. My failure definitely was, in part, due to my unwillingness to help myself. But an eating disorder program that does not require the patients to eat strikes me as particularly futile and pointless. I realize, though, that I certainly didn't give the doctors a lot to work with. Though I had admitted laxative use on my intake survey, I never let on quite how many I took, or how frequently I took them. Right before I left Atlanta, I was drinking about three pots of very strong coffee each day, plus several diet sodas. Hospital regulations did not condone either of these behaviors. While I could understand the prohibitions against laxatives, I rather resented the other restrictions. The geyser of caffeine that had previously energized my weak body was cut off at the source, and, for the first half of my stay, I was rendered essentially catatonic due to sheer caffeine withdrawal.

Part of the problem, too, lay in the newness of their program (I was inpatient numero tres). Most treatment centers that have been around for a while have any number of bizarre rules relating to meal-time and food. At these centers, everyone probably wonders precisely what past patients had done that made for strange rules about eating utensils and baggy sweatshirts and the number of napkins per meal. At Rogers, we were the guinea pigs, and we scurried through each and every loophole we could find. In no time at all, I found more than enough loopholes to appease my eating disorder.

Rogers allotted certain privileges to its residents based on a "level" system. If you behaved yourself, followed the program, and, in the case of eating disordered patients, ate the food, you were allowed to wear shoes with laces and walk around the compound. Accompanied by an omnipresent staff member, of course. It doesn't sound like much, but by the end of the second day, patients were typically ready to sell their souls in exchange for a fifteen-minute walk. I knew this form of "exercise" didn't burn off a significant number of calories, but I enjoyed being out in the fresh air. That, and it provided the perfect opportunity for me to dispose of food from that day's meals.

During mealtimes, when no one was watching, I would take whatever food I didn't want to eat and cram it into my jeans pocket. On our daily walks, I sauntered around the garden out back, hands jammed in my pockets, fingers rubbing over the contraband. I looked around—anyone watching? Yes? I would find something intriguing in a rosebush, bend down to take a whiff. I watched our jailer (excuse me, assigned staff member) out of the corner of my eye. Coast was clear. Now. I would make my move, surreptitiously wriggling handfuls of rice, bread, raisins, and eggs out of my pockets in a series of carefully rehearsed steps. First, I would reach into my pocket, selecting a few scraps of pita bread or raisins or whatever. Then I coughed and raised my fist to my mouth, gaze darting around the garden. Finally, I would bring my hand back down to my side and drop the food, letting it land with a satisfactory splat on the flower beds. I hoped the birds and rabbits were hungry. I inhaled the damp summer air, closed my eyes, *steady now, you're fine, you made it, you did it.* I snickered to myself. Didn't these people know *anything*?

What's more, the staff at Rogers took our word for what we had claimed to eat. At most places, they know you will lie. An eating disorder is not, after all, a disease that lends itself particularly well to honesty. To counteract this, most treatment centers have a staff member check every nook and cranny on your tray for food that has miraculously found a way to escape being eaten. They search through your napkins, shake your cartons of 2% milk, examine the containers of yogurt. Not here. I would pour half of my little box of Rice Krispies into a Styrofoam bowl, pull the foil top of my yogurt back, dump half of it onto the cereal, and mix, making sure to leave a generous coating on the walls of the bowl. No one ever noticed the cereal still in the box and the yogurt carefully hidden under the now-unfolded foil top. And I dutifully reported to staff that I had eaten one box of cereal and one carton of yogurt. Each day, the gap between what I actually ate and what I said I ate widened. At first, my neat little menus were a reasonable approximation of the truth. By the end, my actual daily food intake dropped to six hundred calories per day. I was maintaining a starvation diet in an inpatient program. What a crock.

After the first few meals, I got bored of simply sitting in front of my tray for the required hour, so I began to do rather interesting things with my food. Not that I wasn't already neurotic about anything that wasn't lettuce, but my actions grew from being a personal idiosyncrasy to the object of much curiosity and concern to the other people on the unit. Looking back, I realize that my actions were primarily motivated out of the fear that I would break down and actually take a bite more than I had intended. Playing with food is a hallmark of starvation, though this didn't occur to me at the time. The brain will literally override all sensibilities to encourage you to be around food as much as humanly possible. You will draw out your mealtimes as long as possible. You will shred your piece of pita bread into a thousand tiny pieces, creating a little mountain of pita on your plate. You will eat your peas one at a time with your knife. You will order desserts you have no intention of touching just to smell them, to *experience* them, devouring them in your head. And when you go to bed, you will dream about food while you sleep. Your body is screaming that it needs fuel, but the anorexic somehow manages to override all of these failsafes.

Sanity does, however, occasionally prevail. Three or four days into my stay at Rogers, I found myself, at the urging of one of the other patients, eating all of my dinner, scraping my plate clean. It was some type of pasta dish with chicken, a fairly innocuous substance and one that was above par from what the kitchen usually sent up.

"Ohmygod… I can't believe I just did that." A vise of anxiety tightened around my chest. Surely everyone here thought I was a pig. Looking back, I realize everyone was probably pleased I had finished my plate for once, instead of making an art project out of it, hiding it, or simply leaving it to rot. It was strange, some small part of me, the small, remaining sane portion of myself, the part that had been sub-merged for so long and had finally worked its way to the surface for a quick breath of air before being submerged again, was proud of what I had done. I wanted to run up and down the hallways screaming, "I finished my dinner! I actually *finished* my *dinner*!"

When the psychiatrist came by on his rounds later that evening, I told him what I had done. He looked at me, then stood up, walked over to the window, and looked out.

"Everything's still here."

"What?"

"The world. It's still here. It didn't end when you took your last bite of pasta."

I blinked. What the hell was *that* supposed to mean?

"In fact," he went on, "I didn't even feel it shake."

I stared at my shoe, looked up, shrugged my shoulders.

"Have you ever committed a crime?" he asked me. "I mean a serious one, not just speeding or anything, but like homicide or grand larceny."

"Not that I can recall."

"And are you aware that, even in prisons, where one of the major purposes is to punish people who have done that and worse, American law requires that they be fed regularly?"

"I guess so."

"So what have you done that requires a punishment of this magnitude? You already said you hadn't killed anyone or stolen any-thing, so what is your crime?" He looked intently at me.

I shrugged my shoulders again. "Being born?"

"That's hardly a crime."

"Okay, so what have I done to deserve to eat?" I countered, as I tried to back him into a corner.

"What have any of us done?"

It's wrong, I wanted to say. You just don't *understand*. None of you get it. Instead, I shrugged my shoulders one last time and we simply agreed to disagree. By the time the doctor had completed his rounds, it was almost time for evening snack. I politely declined mine, saying I was still full (which, actually, I sort of was), but staff made me take an apple anyway.

I especially liked the hard-boiled egg whites I usually got for my evening snack, because the shells provided all sorts of opportunities for fun. Though I would leave the inner membrane intact, I would pulverize the shell and pick each tiny piece of calcium carbonate off the said membrane, scattering them around my bowl. My roommate watched me, perplexed, as I prepared my egg. "What," she asked, "in the *hell* are you doing to that thing?" I took the egg, popped out the yolk, and scraped every trace of yellow from the white. I nibbled at the rubbery white that I had shredded into bite-sized pieces. My eyes would dart around to make sure no one was watching while I discreetly mixed tiny portions of the egg white in with my hill of eggshell. Sometimes I got caught; sometimes I didn't. I didn't know whether staff failed to communicate with each other, or were just plain stupid, but, regardless, I took full advantage of this security lapse.

I celebrated my twenty-first birthday on the third floor of Rogers Memorial Hospital, two days after I was admitted. "That must have sucked," Sara said, over the phone. It did, but, to tell you the truth, I found myself secretly relieved. Here, no one would make me eat a piece of cake or have an alcoholic drink, both of which basically contained "empty" calories, nothing I wanted in *my* body.

At dinner that night, since I was still being served on trays brought up to the unit, some of the other patients banded together and made a baked potato "birthday cupcake" look-alike. They frosted it with ranch dressing, wrote "Happy Birthday" in big letters with black pepper, and stuck a plastic straw-turned-candle into the top. It was rather sweet of them, especially considering I had just arrived. They also had another thing right—they said that, considering why I was there, it would have been a slap in the face to give me a piece of "real" birthday cake. I thanked them for their gift, in more ways than one.

On my birthday, I also petitioned (begged, really, though I still hate to admit I stooped that low) the head psychiatrist to have Diet Coke privileges for the women on the unit, in lieu of a birthday party. "*Please?* Just this once? I'm turning *twenty-one*," I pleaded. I wanted to add that being stuck in this hellhole was punishment enough to deal with, especially on such a milestone birthday. He reluctantly agreed, though we weren't allowed access to the cans themselves (you never know—we could cut ourselves). And so a doctor's order was written for that evening's snacktime. All of the women with eating disorders, the whole bony crew of us, spent the day in eager anticipation of bliss in a can. Our aspartame-starved brains practically reeled in excitement.

At the designated time, we lined up at the nurses' station. "*What* are you all doing here?" a nurse, Charmaine, asked.

"We're having Diet Cokes for my birthday," I told her with a grin, cracking my first smile in nearly a week.

"No, you aren't."

"Um, yes, we are."

"I don't think so."

"We had doctor's orders. *Doctor's orders.* Look in my chart. *Look!*" I cried.

Charmaine shook her head. "I see that. But you still can't have Diet Cokes unless you're watched for an hour afterward."

"Why would we purge Diet Coke? There's nothing *in* it. We're allowed to have water without being watched. Why not Diet Coke?" My voice cracked. All I wanted was a stupid can of Diet Coke for my birthday—couldn't these people *see* that?

"Rules are rules," she shrugged.

I lost it. Entirely. The girl who prides herself on never crying in public.

I ran down the hallway, face in my hands, sobbing, back to my room.

"Hey—what's going on?" a different nurse, Tracy, asked, gently grabbing my elbow. "Why are you so upset?" I explained the whole story, sobbing and gasping for air, a haze of snot and tears, blubbering something about "Diet Coke" and "Charmaine." She gently patted me on the back. "I'll see what I can do," she said. I just sniffled.

We ended up getting our Diet Cokes, though by that point, the evening had been ruined. My nose was so clogged from crying that the soda really didn't have any taste. It was months until I was able to face a can of diet soda without shuddering. But that night sealed the friendship between us women on the unit. We had asserted ourselves and won, even though I broke down in the process. The other women on the floor had seen me at my worst—now I didn't have to hide anything from them. Bit by bit, I began to trust.

Another fixture of psych wards is herbal tea—I don't know, maybe they just figure we crazies need to relax. We certainly do, but it's not really polite to point that out. Eating disordered patients in particular are limited to decaf because caffeine is an appetite suppressant and a heart stimulant. Staff also specifically rations the tea because of the tendency we have to use it as a filler. Since this idea had not really occurred to me before I arrived, I took their suggestion and drank cup after cup of weak tea. Weak because we were only allowed two bags per day, and I made my two bags last a *very* long time.

Residents without eating disorders were allowed access to things like sugar packets and sweeteners. We could use sugar, too, if we didn't mind being locked out of our bathrooms for an hour after we finished. I did mind this, thought it very degrading, so I decided to suffer with plain tea. Our lives as patients, *sans* diet soda, existed in sharp contrast to the beverage choices of the nurses. Most drank soda of some sort, usually Diet Coke. I began to see the double standard that existed on the unit and brought it up with one of the nurses after dinner one day. I asked her why it was perfectly acceptable for her to drink Diet Coke, but something of a mortal sin for me.

She looked me right in the eye and drawled, "Honey, I'm not an anorexic."

I glanced at her expansive hips and massive butt. Well, I could see *that*. I said nothing.

"When," I asked, "do you think I will be able to start drinking Diet Coke again?"

"I dunno," she shrugged. "When you're recovered you won't feel the need to drink diet drinks anymore." I wanted to slap her across the face and yell, *But you don't have an eating disorder and you drink Diet Coke and it's all okay for you.* Instead I just *hmmmph*ed in supposed agreement and left the situation alone.

What I didn't realize at the time was that I had stumbled onto one of the dirty little secrets of eating disorder units everywhere. Some of the nurses who work in eating disorder facilities are not—how shall I put this—without pathological eating habits of their own. Many of the caregivers to whom we have entrusted our lives are on an intimately familiar basis with eating disorder symptoms. Some will admit this; most will not. They will not see you for the pathetic specimen that you are. Instead, they admire, sometimes openly, your dual drives toward self-denial and destruction, leaving you wondering why you're in the hospital anyway.

My brain, being driven nearly insane by idly surveying the constant stream of Diet Coke cans that passed through the unit, began to concoct a plan to filch some of the little blue packets of Equal from behind the nurses' station. I enlisted my roommate, a girl my age named Liz. Liz also suffered from a NutraSweet addiction, and was a more-than-willing accomplice.

Having staked out the nurses' station, we knew that the little packets of Equal were kept in a basket behind the carafe of coffee (decaf, of course). The newspapers, our lone link to the outside world, were also kept next to the coffee, and I began my slow infiltration of the area by standing and reading the newspapers in place. I stared at the pages of newsprint, keeping a watch on the nurse out of the corner of my eye. I rested my hand on the counter. Slowly, slowly. Then, once he had turned his head, I made my move. My hand shot out, quick as lightning, snatched a few packets, and shoved them into my jeans pocket. I went back to reading the newspaper, poured myself a cup of coffee, then wandered away. Once back in my room, I counted how many packets I had managed to steal, stashing all but one in a dirty sock. I ripped open the packet of Equal and dumped it into the coffee (which was also contraband, though somewhat less so than the sweetener). I then shoved the empty blue wrapper into the mate of the aforementioned sock. Liz and I split the packets of Equal between us, a stock that kept us both high on aspartame during our stay.

It was, all in all, a rather clever little operation. Until, of course, I got caught.

A throat cleared behind me as I stared blankly ahead at the business section of the paper, my hand resting on the little basket of Equal. "Precisely what," I heard a male voice say, "are you doing?"

This couldn't possibly look good. "Ummm…" I stammered. "Reading the newspaper?" I suggested weakly, grinning sheepishly. He knew I was full of it.

"Uh-huh. Put the packets back."

"Packets of what?" I asked innocently, giving him puppy dog eyes. Most of the time, this worked for me. This wasn't most of the time. He was unmoved.

"Just put them back."

I sighed, gave in, put them back into the basket and sauntered off, head bowed, pretending to sniffle. In reality, a smile played on my lips because I still had about ten packets left in my sock drawer. He thought he had won this little battle. Haha—who would have the last laugh? As it turned out, the nurse would. He evidently let it be known to the rest of the staff that I was stealing sweetener *and* coffee, and the carafes of coffee were thenceforth removed. Shit. Well, so much for that. I consoled myself with the fact that I still had my herbal tea, a fact that didn't make my sudden departure from decaf black coffee any easier.

The rules for the eating disordered patients, the rules which I so flagrantly, brazenly violated, were set by the director of the program. At our first meeting, he introduced himself to me, though I quickly mutated his name to Dr. Weasel. He handed me a pink workbook informatively titled "Overcoming Anorexia Nervosa."

"What's this?" I asked.

"I want you to work on this," he explained slowly. "Each time we meet, we can talk about the pages you completed." Oh. I get it. Busy work. Great. All of my parents' money was funding a stack of workbook pages. Well, hallelujah, praise the Lord. If this doesn't make me want to recover, I don't know what will.

Dr. Weasel laced his fingers together behind his head and leaned back in his chair. "Well."

I decided to be a brat. "Well what?"

He sighed. "How are you?"

I shrugged. You took my coffee away, you *bastard*. How do you *think* I'm doing, you egotistical piece of *shit*? "Fine."

"You're still not in full compliance with the meal plan." No shit, Sherlock.

"I'm trying." He nodded, clearly not impressed. "I'm eating more than when I came in here." At that point, it would have been hard to eat *less*, though I neglected to point that out. Can I *go* already, or are you going to make me listen to more of this theoretically inspirational crap?

"You need to lead the way into recovery." I scoffed at that one. You have *got* to be kidding me. There is no way in hell I was going to let myself get fat. I debated telling him no, that I'd rather lead the charge of the light brigade buck-naked than eat normally again. Instead, I smiled and nodded. Sure, whatever you say, buddy. I swung my leg back and forth, trying to burn off the calories in the low-cal salad dressing I had eaten at lunch. I could try taco sauce on my lettuce. How many calories were in a packet of taco sauce? Less than in Kraft Fat-Free Ranch, I'll bet.

"You know," I said, "if you let us have Diet Cokes when we eat everything on our trays, you could probably get us to eat more." Since I was now in charge of what I put on my tray, I'd just eat one hundred percent of a lot less food.

He nodded, writing something on my chart. Probably something like, *Patient uncommunicative, going through painful diet soda withdrawal.* "Is that all?"

"Yes." No. I have twenty packets of sweetener hidden in my sock right now. Wanna hear about that? Or about the glass of Diet Pepsi I managed to snag in the cafeteria last night? My brain did somersaults of pure ecstasy as the Nutrasweet hit my bloodstream. It was positively orgasmic. I stood up and shook the Good Doctor's hand, humming my personal little ode to aspartame. I was careful how I walked so that the blue packets didn't make any crinkly sounds and give away my secret. I was then herded straight into group therapy.

Throughout each one of my hospital stays, I had trouble taking group therapy seriously. A cadre of adults all sitting around talking about how they're *feeling* and how they're *working* on their *problems* and getting in touch with their inner children was a little too much for me to swallow. By and large, I slept through the group sessions because I didn't think them worth my (or anyone else's) time. I saw us as no more than a group of hopeless screw-ups, too warped for any cheesy therapy sessions. As I would later learn during my day treatment program back home in Detroit, I was wrong, though I still haven't been able to shake that initial mind-set.

When they split everyone up into two groups for our therapy sessions, Rogers lumped the eating disorder patients with the other addicts on the unit. I didn't understand this at first. I understood their interpretation of an eating disorder as another type of addiction, but when I looked at the former cocaine addicts with big, bulging muscles, and then over at us eating disorder patients, our bones sticking out at all these funny angles, I wondered what in the hell they were thinking. Most of them had tattoos and wore grungy white tank tops with black leather motorcycle jackets; the most rebellious thing any of us had done was pierce her nose.

As it turns out, we didn't look a thing alike, but eating disorders *are* an addiction (at least in part) and we all had something to learn from each other. Once we learned not to be intimidated by their bulk, and once they learned we were in no danger of snapping in two, we all came to realize that our issues were the same: feelings of inadequacy and emptiness, anger at the world, confusion about where our lives were supposed to lead. In response, we had all turned to some rather self-destructive behavior, and it slowly began to dawn on us that there just might be a better way to deal with things. Maybe some of these doctors *did* know what they were talking about.

Then again, maybe they didn't.

After several days of togetherness with the substance abuse patients, I rapidly learned what the staff wanted to hear us say. And the faster you spewed out all of the ridiculous nonsense they believed was a prerequisite to surviving in the outside world, the faster you could go home and back to your meals of Diet Coke and baby carrots. To this day, I'm not sure whether they saw through my act, splendid though it was, or if they just went along with my stories to humor me. I slipped through the cracks regardless, so, in the end, I guess it doesn't really matter.

I started my little show for the staff first thing in the morning, and I kept it up until lights out at night. During breakfast, we set our goal for the day, what we hoped to accomplish in group and individual therapy. I usually made up something about trying new foods, not obsessing about food and exercise. I never had any real intention of reaching these goals, but I knew they sounded good on paper. One of my specialties, it seemed, was telling people what they wanted to hear. Almost every word that fell from my lips was a load of male cow excrement, but this never occurred to anyone on staff. Every morning we "checked in" with one another, found out how everyone's day was going. I spoke eloquently of coming face to face with my inner demons and conquering them. Each group member had my full support on the road to recovery. Eating disorder patients are, as a general rule, extremely supportive of one another's recovery efforts, because we are all contending for the prize of "Sickest Anorexic." We forget that the top prize is, in reality, death.

"Remember," Anne had told me as I protested the need for inpatient treatment, "the best anorexics are the dead ones."

This must not have escaped me entirely, because soon I was scribbling poems about death and dying. I wanted so badly to be the best anorexic that I was willing to pay the price.

Riding the Number 20

We passed my stop.
I ring the bell,
signal the driver—
I want to get off.
"Can't stop here, miss,"
the driver shouts.
"I'll let you off
just right up here."
But this is my stop
and I want to leave now.
I have stayed on too long
and I need to get off.
The drunkard leers
at me again from his
precarious perch at
the back of the bus.
Gasoline fumes spin
my head in circles.
I have been on too long

and it is time to leave.
As the bus grinds
slowly to a halt,
I hitch my backpack
up onto my shoulders.
I stumble to the front
and barely catch myself
from falling forwards as
the doors finally open.

Two weeks later, and not a moment too soon, it was time for my parents to come pick me up. I knew I had lost a lot of weight since they had last seen me, and I didn't quite know what to say when I saw them. The night before, I tossed and turned, hunting for the right words. "Surprise, Mom! Your daughter is nucking futs!" would probably not go over too well. But I didn't know what else to say. Besides, I didn't think I looked *that* different, so I passed off the changes due to my eating disorder as only "cosmetic," nothing really all that drastic. With that, I fell into a restless sleep.

The next morning, I played with my breakfast, nibbling at the ubiquitous English muffin coated with a thin layer of sugar-free jelly. I remember constantly pulling up my baggy jeans that had a bad habit of falling down around my butt, and debating with the other women on the floor what shirt to wear. I stuffed a brown fisherman's hat on my head and paced the hallways, waiting for the moment of truth to arrive. I sat down, pretended to read. I glanced up when I heard a door open. I grinned and waved at my mother. She gasped, tried not to show her shock and disbelief at my appearance.

I didn't quite understand what she was so horrified about. Just that morning, one of the social workers had told me how much better I was looking than when I arrived. To me, I was the same person I had always been. The physical alterations of anorexia simply hadn't registered with me, and though I no longer saw "fat," I sure as hell didn't see "thin." Maybe I had just gotten used to the sunken eye sockets and protruding cheekbones. My lower jaw appeared permanently thrust forward and my lower lip pulled tightly over my front teeth in a hideous approximation of a feral grin. My skin stretched tight over each and every bone. My spine ended in a protruding bony mass upon which I could rest my hands and arch my back. I didn't have anything that would qualify as a butt anymore, only a small section of flesh dipping inwards instead of curving gently out.

"I almost didn't recognize you," my mom said later. "You were positively *gray*. I felt like we had just broken you out of Auschwitz."

Personally, I thought my appearance as a walking jumble of skin and bones was just the look I was going for. I even thought I could certainly stand to lose five more pounds. When I arrived home, I rather deliberately changed into a tank top and boxer shorts, just to see if I could finally see some physical changes myself. My mom stared at me as I emerged from the bathroom. She didn't say anything, but her eyes were wild with fear. Here was her child, gleefully knocking on death's door, ringing the doorbell, then running and hiding to see if anyone opened it. And she had no choice but to sit and watch and pray to God that her daughter didn't get caught.

I remember her hugging me gently, softly, afraid I would break if she squeezed too hard (I realize now that this was the same way I hugged Amy before I left Rogers). She then ran her hands over the back of my rib cage, counting each bone, each vertebrae, measuring how much each protruded. Each day the hugs got a little softer, and the bones sharper.

My parents had made appointments for me with an eating disorder physician and a nutritionist, both of whom I saw immediately upon returning home. I didn't really see the point of all this, since I had no intention of changing what I was doing, regardless of what a doctor might tell me. I went, however, because it was easier than arguing about *not* going. I sat in the waiting room with my mother and refused to fill out any health history forms or other such documents. I saw the medical profession as the enemy, and when my name was called, I steeled my jaw to prepare for battle with the hated doctor. This one used a new tactic on me; she tried to scare me out of restricting.

"If you keep going like this, you could have a heart attack," she told me levelly, gravely. Her brown eyes locked on my green ones. "You could die." Oh, please, God, don't let me laugh. I pressed my lips tightly together, determined not to crack a grin. This was piteous—who was she kidding. Me? Have a heart attack? Heart attacks were for old, portly men with beer bellies, not a twenty-one-year-old college student. Besides, lots of models were skinnier than me and no one was harping at *them* to gain weight.

"Can I see your stomach?" I lifted my eyebrows and my shirt. She ran her hand over the soft downy fuzz that now covered my trunk. "Feel this?" I nodded. "That's called *lanugo*. Your body makes it when you're starving, in order to keep you warm. You need to get more nutrients." Yeah, well, I needed a million bucks, too, and I didn't see that happening any time soon, either. But I told her that I understood and that I would try.

I laced my shoes and turned to go. "Twenty percent of people with eating disorders die. That's one out of every five of my patients. Those are your odds. Think about it." Then, she shook my hand and walked out. I just shrugged my shoulders.

The nutritionist, a wonderful Italian woman named Patrizia, was charged with the monumental task of dismantling my food fears, bite by bite. We started with a checklist of common foods, and I indicated whether I would or wouldn't eat them. To an anorexic, food is never as simple as yes or no. I had to qualify many of the items I checked off, such as "yogurt," with phrases like "sugar-free, fat-free *only*, 100 cals/ carton." Beside "milk" was *"only* skim, *only* a dribble in first cup of coffee." Just about the only foods that didn't have qualifiers were the vegetables. I even added my own category, "Condiments," since a large portion of the calories I ate came from mustard, artificial sweetener, Mrs. Dash, and coffee grounds.

I handed my annotated list back to Patrizia and she paged through it. She didn't say anything at first, and then she asked, "What about protein? Don't you eat any protein?" I thought about that for a second. "Nope. Guess not," I replied. So my goal for the first week was to incorporate a protein source into my diet. Patrizia suggested peanut butter; I suggested tuna fish. I would end up eating neither.

I felt downright naked in those first few sessions with Patrizia. I never had any intention of introducing anyone to the world of Carrie's Food, and it seemed as if the most private part of me was now displayed on a billboard beside a busy interstate. I had a stake in keeping this world private, too. If my beliefs were challenged and I began to question them, the foundation of my world would crack. I couldn't afford to let a nutritionist into my world and risk losing my eating disorder.

My return from Rogers cloaked an already edgy house in utter fear. I was terrified of many things, mainly of eating and gaining weight, but I also had a sobering vision of myself at thirty-one, eating five celery sticks with mustard and Mrs. Dash for dinner, and the thought of remaining in this hell for that long scared me, too. I worried about my parents—I thought I was eating enough and that I wasn't really all that sick, but I was afraid they had some Doomsday scenario all played out in their minds. I had my own, more selfish, motives behind this fear as well. If my parents thought my condition had deteriorated *too* far, they might just send me back to the hospital where they would fatten me up for sure.

With all of these fears pinging around in my head, I felt enormous pressure to return to "normal." Part of the problem, though, was that I couldn't remember what normal was in the first place. Besides, "normal" in my eyes was rather different than what, for instance, my mother might think. This problem was compounded by the fact that many of my bizarre eating behaviors were biochemically driven, either by OCD or starvation. I ate pickle relish right from the jar, would sneak spoonfuls of jelly or a dollop of Cool Whip when no one was watching. For one dinner, I remember eating two leftover stale pizza crusts. Even my eating implements turned strange. I stopped using spoons and forks and knives like normal people. Everything I ate just *had* to be consumed with a baby-sized feeding spoon, and if I couldn't figure out a way to use one, then I simply wouldn't eat.

It was during this time that I discovered fake butter. Up until my release from Rogers, I did not know there was such a thing, would not have even fathomed its existence. But on one of my wide-eyed wanderings through the grocery store, I happened across a tub of I Can't Believe It's Not Butter—Fat Free. "Only five calories per serving!" the label at the bottom bragged. Well, fancy that. I could indulge in the decadence of butter completely guilt-free. Hot damn! I bought a tub, just for kicks, figuring if I hadn't already poisoned myself with fake food, a little bit of imitation butter wasn't going to put me over the top. I pretended to buy it for family use, but I knew it was only going to be used by me. Its presence seemed almost to mock me from inside the fridge.

One afternoon, I smuggled the container up to my room, pried off the lid, closed my eyes, and inhaled the rich buttery scent. I took my little baby spoon and scraped a shaving of butter off the top. *Mmmmmm...* Double-checking to make sure no one would interrupt my bonding episode with imitation buttery chemicals, I proceeded to relish every last molecule in the container. My taste buds thoroughly titillated, I closed my eyes, savoring the sweet creamy aftertaste and smooth texture. I opened my eyes. What the hell just happened? What on God's green earth had I *done*? I stared at the yellow plastic, realized in horror I had just consumed an entire tub of I Can't Believe It's Not Butter. The little container said "Only five calories per serving," but, sweet mother of God, how many servings had I just eaten? The tub had to contain *at least* 150 calories—that was like eating *two whole slices* of bread. Shit. What was I going to do? What the hell was I going to do? Quick—hide the spoon. I shoved it into my pocket.

I realized I was going to have to explain the empty carton at dinnertime. I panicked. My greatest fear, at this point, was not that I was so starved I could eat a pound of fake butter and not think it odd, but that my family would discover I had eaten a pound of fake butter and think I was a pig. So I snuck out of the house, spoon in tow, ostensibly returning some books to the library, but instead went to the grocery store, where I bought another tub of fake butter. In the parking lot, I scraped the top layer off so it would look like I had eaten some, then smuggled it back into the house in my (large) purse.

To this day, I don't know whether or not anyone in my family figured out I was eating fake butter on the sly. It sounds ridiculous, that I would peck at a container of imitation butter like a starved sparrow, but, like so many other things I've done, it sounded like a good idea at the time. Never once did it occur to me that had I not been so nutritionally deprived, I would *not* have eaten a tub of I Can't Believe It's Not Butter. If anyone had caught me, it would have given away my little secret, the one upon which my eating disorder hinged—I was hungry. Terribly, ravenously hungry, though I would have died (indeed, I almost did) before I admitted it.

I had honed my deception skills to a fine point while in the hospital, and I was eager to try them out on my unsuspecting family once I got out. Every night, before I went to bed, I would draw up a list of what I was going to eat the next day. If I had been "extra good" that day, I would graciously allow myself little extras, say a nibble of pretzels or a peanut. Yes, you read right. One peanut. Just one. One lone Mr. Planter. I clearly marked which foods I was going to eat, which ones I would pretend to eat, and which ones I would plainly not touch, as well as when I would eat them. At any rate, I figured my going to get a snack and walking off with it would probably fool my parents and save them from coming to offer me food. As it turns out, I was right.

So at the designated time, I wandered innocently into the kitchen, and would pour myself a mini-bowl of cereal or throw two Eggos into the toaster. When I had finished preparing the food, most of which I had no intention of eating, I took the obligatory nibble in front of my parents. "Yum, isn't this *good*?" I would exclaim, as I gathered up my snack. Into the baggie I had stashed in my desk drawer went the dry cereal or pretzels, bit by bit, so that it appeared I was actually nibbling on them throughout the day. When I had filled the little Zip-Loc bag to capacity, I stuffed it into my purse and threw it away the next time I was out by myself. I had devised quite an elaborate food smuggling factory, one that worked exceedingly well.

I didn't enjoy doing this, for several reasons. One, I wasn't oblivious to the wasted food and the amount I disposed of on a daily basis didn't sit too well on my conscience. Two, I blamed my parents for making me throw food away. If they would just get *off* my case for *two minutes* about *eating*, then I *wouldn't* have to *do* this. After all, when I was in Atlanta, I never threw food away, not on this scale. Three, the perpetual lying began to eat at me. I didn't like it, didn't like how the lies so easily rolled off my tongue and how frequently I found myself having to deceive those who loved me. Yet I still viewed it as a necessary evil.

I was not, to put it mildly, happy to be home. I did not celebrate being in the warm bosom of my family, nor was I eager to have such a wonderful support system cheering me on. It was rather the opposite. I felt hemmed in, claustrophobic, like the baby chick whose mother hen sits on her all day. The presence of so much loving kindness drowned me with wave after wave of guilt—I knew my goal of ultimate starvation and thinness was death, and I had accepted the price. The fewer people who cared, the less guilt I would carry as I starved myself to death. Nothing, it appeared, held enough meaning to pull me out of the death trap called anorexia.

At summer's end, while I was packing to return to Hope, I couldn't shake the feeling that my parents were conspiring *behind my back* to try and take away my eating disorder. My fears were confirmed one night, two days before I left, when my parents sat me down for a "conversation." Dear Lord—I managed to wriggle my way out of the infamous birds and bees talk as a kid, only to fall victim to something much, much worse now. My parents' efforts, valiant though they were, fell on deaf ears. Anorexia was *my* little thing and no one was going to take it away from me.

"What's going to happen to you once you get back to school? What then?" demanded my father. "What if you continue on the path you're on?" His voice cracked and a knife twisted horribly, violently, in my chest. My father never cried.

I said, "Don't worry. Please don't worry. I'm fine. It will all be fine. You'll see."

I thought, I'm not even that sick right now.

I thought, What is he going to do once I really get the

ball rolling?

I did not know, of course, that the ball was already careening out of control.

But I guarded myself against any grandiose displays of emotion and rather petulantly replied that I was fine, perfectly fine, would you people stop *worrying* for five minutes? Nothing was going to happen. You just have to trust me, you *never* trust, I squawked indignantly.

I am haunted, still, by how right my parents were, and how very wrong I proved myself to be.

Hungering, I
go out, I
go ravening into the woods
feed me, I cry
to the trees, desire
rising driven
in me like
a sap and falling
into my body again
I enter into the world
eating the snow, this
is my breath, I
say air of us feeding
me look
at this acorn I made
Love, to know you
like this, flesh
bound as I am, you
in your ecstasy
branching, I
in my green thoughts
growing up
out of the snow.

Kim Chernin, "The Hunger Song"

Chapter Six: The Hunger Song
Hope College, September 2001

I arrived at Hope with the grim intention of battling with my body to pursue the outer limits of Hunger, Insanity, and Death. I don't think, at that point, I had the presence of mind to contemplate finishing the semester, though I do remember thinking that I would lose more weight if I remained in school. So back to Hope I went, not realizing how much further I had to fall before I finally reached rock bottom and not understanding how hard that fall would be once it came.

I ran into one of my roommates, Liz, as I began to unload the boxes from my car. She stared at me for a long minute. I thought she was admiring my weight loss. I thought she was secretly jealous of my ability to starve.

"Carrie," she told me later, "I didn't recognize you. I stared at your face and wondered, 'Who *is* that girl over there?' Then I realized, oh, dear Lord—that's Carrie."

My appearance during the short time I managed to stay at Hope must have been ghastly. I know for a fact that debates flew among my friends as to whether I had cancer or (this one still strikes me as humorous) AIDS. No one said anything directly to my face, and I would have denied it if anyone had. I focused my intentions on buffering myself with solitude so that no one would have the chance to ask questions. As anorexics continue to starve themselves, sex hormones cease to be produced in the brain, causing, among other things, amenorrhea (the cessation, temporary or otherwise, of menstruation), thyroid malfunction, and a decreased sex drive. Interestingly enough, this also causes an inability to communicate and interact with other people. Our brains are literally too starved to relate to other human beings.

Starvation sounds so romantic, so dainty and birdlike and I'm-a-goddess-because-I-can-pick-at-my-dinner-plate-in-pure-saintliness. This whole myth makes me want to vomit. We hear of these stories of miraculous medieval women who fasted for years on end, earning the respect of a very patriarchal society.[12] Even today, we still think that starvation is some wonder-of-the-Lord phenomenon, and society tries to repeat these feats, over and over, year after year. But God does not want people living in the Land of Plenty to die of hunger. Starvation and anorexia are neither pretty nor saintly, not the idealized wasting away that the Victorians would have us believe.

Rather than being surrounded with halos and angels bawling hymns in their praise, anorexics in the late stage of their disease look rather horrific, quite the opposite of the embodiment of sainthood and health. Your hair, no matter how healthy and thick and lustrous it may have been before you started losing weight, will turn dank and dull. It will start falling out, first strand by strand, then in huge hunks, getting stuck in your fingers as you rake them across your scalp. After you have littered your hairbrush and the bathroom floor with hair, you will gaze into the mirror at your too-large eyes, sunken deeply into their sockets, with dark crescents underneath. You will then move on to gaze at the skin stretched taut over the cartilage of your nose. Your cheeks are pinched and tight, so much so that your cheekbones appear far too

---

[12] Rudolph Bell's Holy Anorexia is a good introduction to the concept of fasting during the Middle Ages and the development of the disease now referred to anorexia mirabilis, miraculous anorexia. In her book Fasting Girls, Joan Jacobs Brumberg provides a concise contrast between anorexia nervosa and anorexia mirabilis.

large for your face, and you can even trace the outline of your teeth in your parchment paper skin.

As you continue downward, your eyes catch a glimpse of your collarbones, those wonderful coat hangers for your gaping T-shirt, protruding from your chest. You stretch your shirt tightly over your breasts to see that your curves have slowly straightened into lines. Your breastbone is no longer a level surface, it's a rounded, bumpy little thing now. All the fat has melted away, and your shirts now seem to drip off you like droplets of dew off a dandelion. Extending from your torso like two long and awkward canoe paddles, your wasted arms tremble at the slightest task because you no longer have the strength to do even the simplest of chores. Taking off your shirt, you will lay down on your bed and try to feel your backbone through your stomach. You cannot tell for sure if you're touching it, because your protruding rib cage keeps getting in the way. You run your bluish-gray fingers over the little hills and valleys of your abdomen, feeling each and every bone through your skin. Your hips—ah, the hips! Not soft, round, womanly curves, but instead a pelvis that pokes through the skin, sharp and rigid, creating a sort of bowl where your quiescent ovaries now lay.

Indeed, your whole body looks like it was drawn with a ruler, all straight lines and flat planes. You do not have a butt. The most notice-able feature about your ass is not the ass itself, but rather the tailbone that protrudes from your back. Your legs extend in a straight line down from the hips, widening not at the thighs (Thighs? What thighs? The ones you're convinced you still see each time you stand in front of the mirror…), but instead at the kneecap. Though your kneecap is a natural part of the body, it looks alien on an anorexic, all the joints and tendons sticking out, a bumpy, wiry mass stained purple from both cold and the many bruises you sustain. Even your feet are thinner, your shoes rattling around as you walk. Your body has, in effect, become a shelled-out husk, incapable of sustaining the pittance of a life you have left.

I sensed myself severing all ties with the world and the people who resided in it. I felt I would be leaving soon, and it was time to say good-bye. I grew more and more detached, my world revolving around one thing and one thing only: anorexia. By the end of August, I had stopped kidding myself that I was just "on a diet," just trying to "lose a little weight." I was starving myself, going all-out, pulling out all the stops, trying to see how far I could possibly go.

And when I finally fell, I fell hard.

I was incredibly lucky that someone was there to catch me. I am well aware that not everyone is that fortunate. I am also aware that my "support system," those tenacious, stubborn, and occasionally downright annoying people who stood by my side while I tried and tried to destroy myself, also helped to pick me up off the ground and get me back on my feet again. But a support system doesn't mean squat if you're not a willing participant in the battle against your eating disorder.

I go over and over in my mind what could have happened to me had I not bailed out in Atlanta and agreed to get help at Rogers. Or what disasters might have befallen me had I insisted on staying at Hope. Some part of me desperately wanted to ruin what was left of my health. To this day, I think back on how much more weight I could have lost, how much closer I could have danced with death, and I have to draw myself up short. These are *not* accomplishments, I remind myself, only one more notch in an anorexic's ever-tightening death belt.

ᘓ

Disposables

Kroger advertised plastic knives—
buy one get one free in the
sale ads this week.
"Such a bargain!" I thought
as I
jumped into my Volvo to
beat the masses of people to
the half-off plastic cutlery.
"How amazing!" exclaimed the
woman standing next to me.
"You don't even have to
wash them.
You can eat and then
throw these knives
away."
She picked up a package and
dropped them in her cart,
next to the box of
paper plates
and Dixie cups.

CR

While picking up food for our apartment at Hope, Sara and I run into one of my friends from Scotland. We stop and chit-chat for a few minutes, then, of all things, the conversation turns to weight loss.

"Did you lose a lot of weight or something?" she asks with an air of incredulity. "You look so *thin*."

I forcibly stop myself from thanking her for the compliment, though I can't quite wipe the smile off my face. "Um, sort of."

Before I can get another word out, Sara cuts in with, "She has an eating disorder."

"Oh. I see." Her tone clearly says she doesn't. "How do you do it?"

"Do what?"

"Keep the weight off. How do you do it? Do you just not eat or something? I'm having some trouble with Atkins and I'm looking for some hints."

I am floored. Someone is asking an anorexic, a person with a blatantly obvious, potentially deadly, pathological body image problem, for weight loss tips. To this day, I am still astounded by the ignorance of the general population toward eating disorders. The response of my Scottish friend, though extreme, it seems, is generally representative of society's perspective. People generally believe anorexia is just a normal diet taken a little too far, nothing more.

I beg her, you don't want to go there, believe me, you don't. "You don't need to lose weight. You look *fine* just the way you are," I reassure her, though I fear it falls on deaf ears.

Even at a religious school like Hope, a place where one would think the student body would be above earthly concerns like dress size and calorie counts, eating disorders run rampant. This is, perhaps, in part due to the fact that the underlying cause of eating disorders has absolutely nothing to do with food and weight. One would naturally assume that an appearance-conscious environment would breed more messed-up eating habits than one like Hope, which supposedly focuses on the great hereafter. I say this not to disparage my friends who are ardently searching for truth on this little planet of ours and who also have a few warped ideas about food, but to emphasize how common anorexia and bulimia have become. I can hardly keep count of the number of people that I know with eating disorders at Hope, and it truly astounds me just how prevalent these problems are. Eating disorders almost appear to be contagious. As the number of anorexics and bulimics in Hope's class of 2002 grew, I came to realize I would be among that group.

ଔ

I am transfixed by a cookie.

Routine pit stop at JP's Coffee. Sara accompanies me, orders something. I wrench my brain, happily humming Cookie Monster's theme song, back to reality mode.

Coffee. Bloody pick *something already, you idiot.*

Can I get a flavor shot? I've been good.

Not that *good. Greedy bitch.*

They have three different kinds of sugar free, and it's only five calories, only *five*, come on, please?

I order, asking for sugar-free flavoring, are you *sure* it's sugar free? Positive? I interrogate the girl behind the counter for a full five minutes to be *absolutely certain* she's competent to press the pump on the proper bottle.

Should have skipped the flavoring. They might have accidentally switched labels in the factory, and evil sugar could now be flowing through my veins and racing straight toward my butt. I add four packets of pink sweetener to the Styrofoam cup and try not to think about it.

Sara watches my ritualistic coffee preparations with a profound distaste. I open each packet separately, dump it in, select a plastic stirrer, mix the brew, dispose of the paper and plastic stick, repeat. I examine the little pink packets, horrified to learn each little dose of white powder contains two-and-a-half calories. Oh, shit. How *dare* the company label this as calorie free? In a fit of anger, fueled by fear, I vow to sue them for false advertising. Do people have *any* idea how much of this crap I have consumed over the past few months? Panic-stricken, I vow not to eat anything the next day and run ten extra laps to make up for all of that bloody Sweet 'N Low. Breathe. The knot of anxiety around my stomach loosens. That's better. See? We can always make up for our past mistakes.

Sara approaches me from behind. "Did you get a real coffee drink?"

"It's not like not ordering the real stuff is a crime here or anything," I retort.

"Just as well. If you had one, it would take longer for you to starve yourself to death." I stare after her as she breezes out the door. Could it really be true? Was I really slowly killing myself? Did I truly not fear my own, rather immanent, demise?

The answer was a resounding yes.

My best friend had just resigned herself to my death, a fact that knocked the wind out of me then, as it does now.

Did it knock enough sense into me to start eating? Not quite.

Instead, I struggle to walk back to my apartment, jello legs trembling with every step, muscles attempting to feed on the Tootsie Roll I ate for lunch. Much weaker now. Hands trembling, head spinning, I stumble into my room and concoct another story to help me avoid dinner.

Later that evening, I spy one of Sara's onions lying out on the counter, and decide, at some point, it would be a suitable facsimile of a dinner. I pull half a cucumber out of the crisper, which I slice and dice along with the onion, topping them with salsa, then relish my creation for an hour. Dinner: fifty calories.

It tastes vile. I end up throwing it up, not intentionally, but the concoction of onion, salsa, and cucumber just won't stay *down*. My stomach literally can not digest it, and so I stand, retching, head hung over the kitchen sink, thankful I am once again alone. I still shudder at the taste, and have not brought myself to go near an onion since.

As my eating disorder tightened its vise around my life, I grew more and more neurotic about calorie counting, even rationing chewing gum to one stick per day. I lived in a world where every single calorie counted, and I vowed to keep track of them all. The list of "safe" foods slowly shrunk down to two things: lettuce and tomatoes. Everything else was either off-limits entirely, or eaten only under great protest.

Most anorexics devise elaborate systems of food categories to help them lose weight. Some people will only eat food of a certain color or things that can be consumed out of bowls. In order for me to even consider consuming a food, it had to have an "even" number of calories, a nice, neat little number that could be added or subtracted with ease. I counted in multiples of twenty-five, rounding up to make sure I did not ingest too much. The margins of my textbooks were filled with columns of numbers as I added, subtracted, and multiplied everything that I ate. I got to be *very* good at mental math. After a while, that's basically all I did. I didn't live—I counted calories.

I find, even now, no words exist to describe the mania of that week and a half back at school. I attended lectures. Several pieces of loose-leaf paper attest to that, as do vague memories of frigid lecture halls and impossibly uncomfortable plastic desk chairs. Any more details escape me, even obvious things like the names of my classes. I have textbooks packed in boxes here in my room, chapters neatly highlighted in yellow, occasional notes in the margins. I can identify my handwriting and the system I used to color code my notes, but I cannot tell you how they got there. I simply don't remember. I have homework assignments, graded and returned to me, and though I recognize my work, I have no explanation of how the words appeared on the page. My memory is riddled with more holes than Swiss cheese, and try as I will, I cannot yet fill them in.

After a day or two, I stopped trying to play at being normal, and simply dropped the pretense of pretending to eat. By this time, I knew no one would believe the tales I told anyway, so I figured it just wasn't worth the effort. A surge of cockiness left me with the attitude that people couldn't make me eat regardless, and I threw that in everyone's face each chance I got. Even after only a few short days, I realized that I wouldn't finish the semester. I felt myself dying, and found myself beginning to grasp the very real possibility that my life might conclude before I received my next grade report. And, again, I no longer cared.

My roommates lived normally. One night they ordered Chinese carry-out. They ate their fill and then put the leftovers in the fridge, where the contents softly, seductively called my name, trying to lure me into just a bite. Even the uneaten leftovers beckoned from the trash. I could hear the cold, half-eaten egg roll broadcasting my name on a radio frequency audible only to myself— "I am *so* yummy. You want me. You *know* you want me."

Before I could explain what had come over me, I dug through the garbage can and stuffed my face full of Chinese leftovers. I gasped and sobbed in between each bite, hating each mouthful I gobbled, hating myself even more for breaking down and giving in, yet finding myself unable to stop.

Panic washed over me. I had consumed a maximum of half an egg roll with a few pieces of fried rice clinging to the soggy batter coating. That I hadn't eaten decently in over six months failed to register, nor the fact that I hadn't eaten anything else that day. What had I just done? I ran into the bathroom and bolted the door behind me. A hasty search of my medicine bag produced my last hope—extra-strength Ex-Lax. Sobbing, I swallowed a handful of the little blue pills.

Undo the damage. Gulping air, I braced myself for the pills to do their dirty work and leave me clean.

My knees buckled. I slumped down onto the bathroom floor, laid my head on the cold edge of the toilet, and sobbed. My body could not be denied. That messy, horrible, awful body, demanding to be fed. I had lost control of it. This terrified me more than the food I had just eaten. I thought that if I could fully command my hunger, teach it who was boss, I could be free of my heavy body.

In the short amount of time I spent back at Hope, somewhere in the neighborhood of ten days, I learned first-hand what hell must be like. Most religions conceive of hell as a very large barbeque; my concept of it more resembles the Arctic tundra than Dante's *Inferno*. All I can say for sure was that I was cold. Attempting to do any sort of meaningful work was clearly out of the question for anyone convinced that she was dying of hypothermia on the spot. September in Michigan is not particularly noted for frost and snow, though, at that point, I definitely would have told you otherwise. Teeth chattering, I mindlessly roamed the campus in the seventy-five-degree sunshine, shivering in jeans and a long-sleeved shirt, trying to burn off as many calories as possible while I listened to strains of the chapel service. I praised God for keeping me from eating any calories yet that day, recited a "Hail Mary" for each piece of hard candy I had consumed.

Everywhere I went, I felt like I was wandering around in a large freezer. Regardless of how many layers of clothing I piled on, my body would still shiver. I began to keep my nails painted in order to conceal the perpetual blue tint. I upped the ante on my coffee intake out of sheer desperation to try and warm up. I would do all of this, and still I was cold. Even hot showers failed to banish the chill that numbed me to the bones. My hands trembled constantly, though I cannot say whether that was due to lack of heat or lack of nutrition.

This hell existed in sharp contrast to the lives of my friends around me. They ate real meals. They even ate snacks. And they didn't spend all day reading nutrition labels, wondering whether eating two cherry tomatoes would make their stomachs blimp out. I can remember almost everything I ate during those ten days at Hope. I literally spent all of one Saturday afternoon drowning in sheer panic because I ate forty calories of sugar-free Jell-O. The thought of having anything at all in my body became positively repulsive, and I solemnly renounced food for the rest of my life.

After a while, anorexics genuinely start to believe they don't have to eat. I sublimely believed I did not need food. Other people, maybe. Me? I was special.

Don't get me wrong—I had to be around food constantly. I loved to go grocery shopping, even though I was buying things I would only stare at, not actually eat. I remember several trips to the supermarket during those ten days, and upon entering the store, I fell into a sort of religious trance. FOOD! Aisles and aisles of food. I thought heaven simply had to be God's very own bakery, with piles and piles of yummy, rich, and gooey calorie-free desserts. All for me. I carried food with me in my backpack that I had no intention of eating. I would go to the supermarket every few days, buying huge quantities of things I wouldn't open, just to enjoy the feeling of a full pantry.

Even now, I am still a sitting duck for any kidnapper who happens to be cruising Kroger. I cannot think rationally in a grocery store—there's just too much of everything. Too much variety of too much merchandise in too many aisles. My brain literally goes into sensory overload.

People without eating disorders generally believe anorexics hate food. It's not true. We love food. We eat vicariously by cooking elaborate meals for our friends and family. Just being around food, the mere smell of it, convinces us that we have eaten. Cooking and baking becomes an all-consuming obsession. I had become a walking nutrition fact book. Every waking thought was about food in some form or another, and it followed me even into sleep. I began to dream about food; first chocolate, then, after a while, I moved onto more sundry items, such as cabbage, Brussels sprouts, asparagus, *anything*. The less we eat, you see, the more food consumes us. It has been documented that people in starvation mode have appetites for strange things, even non-nutritive substances. I wolfed down spoonfuls of coffee grounds (did coffee beans have calories?), ate jelly (sugar-free, of course) straight from the jar, squeezed mustard directly into my mouth.

As anorexics continue to starve for weeks and months, the body's level of electrolytes plummets, making us crave sodium in the worst way imaginable. We just *need* to cover *everything* with piles of salt. If it ever came down to it, I would have fought a small child for a salt shaker. Even in my sorry state, I knew that eating straight salt was not a bright idea, so I rummaged through my alphabetically arranged seasonings to find a suitable substitute. Cinnamon, cloves, ginger, nutmeg, oregano, paprika… Mrs. Dash.

I looked at the little bottle of "Classic Italian Seasonings," removed the little yellow cap, took a whiff. I shrugged my shoulders—what the hell—and poured some onto a spoon. I can't really describe the taste, other than strong. Potently strong. My eyes watered furiously, and I spat small pieces of green all over the sink. I swished with water, spat, again and again. I shudder even now at the memory.

I also bought pickles. Jars and jars of pickles. I would eat them like candy, up to one jar per day. I wandered around my apartment toting my trusty jar of pickles, the lone food I would allow myself to be seen consuming. I ate pickles for breakfast, pickles with mustard, even drank pickle juice. The great thing was that each jar only contained a maximum of ten calories. There was a downside to all of those pickles, however—a massive case of indigestion and water retention. Each pickle contained 10 percent of the daily allowance of sodium. Multiply that by twenty pickles per jar, and you have a *lot* of salt. This, compounded by the fact that I really wasn't eating anything else, made me turn into a human water balloon. It would take four pots of *very* strong coffee and several bottles of water before my kidneys readjusted.

Water retention is, however, a particularly convenient phenomenon when one is trying to manipulate one's weight in the upward direction. I was allowed to return to Hope on the condition that I would see Jeanne once a week and have my weight monitored by the student health center. I waltzed into the health clinic for my first weigh-in bloated with pickle juice, water, and pride. I thought I was pretty clever, artificially increasing my weight by several pounds. I had the strange feeling, however, that the nurses knew I was cheating. As I was handed a paper gown to put on before I hopped on the scale, the nurse spoke to me in that calm, gentle, patronizing tone that one uses with terminally ill grandparents.

"Carrie," she sighed, "we both know you can scam your way through this, but you're only hurting yourself if you do." I nodded my head in complete agreement, of course I understood. I informed her of my heartfelt desire to work with Jeanne to stop my continuing weight loss and work toward recovery.

My words were, of course, a load of crap. I hopped on the scale, face-forward, stubborn till the bitter end, determined not to be robbed out of knowing my weight. "Ninety-eight pounds," she announced.

Did I hear her right? Was I really below a hundred pounds again? I felt a surge of triumph—this anorexia thing was *really working*. My weight only had *two numbers* in it. I stifled an exultant yell. "Putting on a few pounds would probably be beneficial. You'll feel better, too."

Feel better, my foot. Gaining weight would make me feel positively bovine, not *better*. The *hell* I'm going to put on a few pounds.

She patted me on the shoulder. "We'll see you next week."

I crumpled up the paper gown and pitched it in the trash. "Oh, and Carrie?" she said. "Do go and see Jeanne in the counseling center." I agreed and smirked to myself.

I immediately trotted upstairs to the track and ran laps for half an hour. Everyone was *so* stupid. How easy was this? No one wanted to believe that the top student in her college class would starve herself to death, so they clung to every scrap of evidence that may have indicated otherwise. I simply told everyone what they wanted to hear, and I could basically do whatever I wanted.

I made my obligatory visit to the counseling center, and chatted with the secretary. "Oh, I'm so *glad* to be back, how about you?" I said, even though my presence in that office said, rather clearly, that *something* in my life wasn't going so hot. I bullshitted just as much with Jeanne as with the nurse, only in less obvious terms. I spoke of my struggles, to be sure, but I countered that with how I was Fighting My Eating Disorder. It was all very grand, in a Capra-esque sort of way, though none of what I spoke about contained a scrap of truth. I based my strategy on the *modus operandi* of my father ("If you can't impress them with your knowledge, dazzle them with your bullshit."), always making my victories less-than-perfect to ensure they were still believable. After a week, I found I had to invent struggles because I wasn't precisely trying, even half-heartedly, to battle my eating disorder. I'm not entirely sure Jeanne believed a word I said, though I think she humored me because she knew my lies would become apparent soon enough. I was convinced I was dying, my lone accurate perception from this time, and I simply did not care. I was going to let myself die, and I told the world to go shove it. One person wouldn't let me.

I had met Amy before, knew her by sight, even interviewed her for the *Anchor*, but we'd never actually spoken informally until I ran into her in the psych nurse's waiting room. We mumbled awkward hellos, both embarrassed to admit we had serious mental health problems. I wondered what was wrong with her, supposed she did the same with me. Except that my condition was a little more obvious at this point. There was no hiding that I was anorexic—even Joe Blow walking down the street could see that I was way too thin. And of course, Amy guessed. I didn't know it at the time, but Amy was intimately familiar with the symptoms of an eating disorder, having struggled with bulimia and anorexia for nine years. She had spent her summer in treatment at Remuda Ranch in Arizona. She mentioned something about an eating disorder support group starting up on campus, and wondered if I wanted to meet for coffee, presumably to talk about our common problems with food. I agreed, figured it couldn't hurt, and then panicked. What on earth was I going to order? Plain black coffee with five packets of artificial sweetener basically screamed "anorexic," and I didn't want her to think I was entrenched in my disorder. Yet I didn't want to order anything besides black coffee because it would have calories. Quite the conundrum.

I solved this little dilemma of mine by starving myself all day, then ordering a small mocha at JP's Coffee, the watering hole for our dry campus. I was torn, strangely, between wanting to lie to Amy and pretend things were okay, and exaggerating my story to make things seem a whole lot more tragic than they really were. I managed, some-how, to do both. I talked about how I used to be sick, very sick, but I'm all better now. I gave her a wistful little smile. Amy softly smiled back. "No, you're not."

"What do you mean I'm not?"

"I mean that you're still very sick. However better you think you may be, however much you may have improved from this summer, you're still sick, sweetie."

I contemplated this. She had a point there.

"Have..." she started, then flushed and stared at her napkin. "Have you ever thought about leaving Hope and getting help?"

Actually, no, I hadn't. I told her this. She nodded in agreement. "I was the same way last spring. Denying your problems won't make them go away."

"I just want to graduate with my friends," I said.

"Talk to some people here. You can work something out."

"I don't know... It's all just too much for me right now."

"Promise me you'll look into it," Amy pleaded.

I capitulated. "All right. I promise." I had no intention of doing anything like that, and I wondered if she knew that as well.

 CR

Wednesday, September 5, 2001. That I remember this date astounds me still. I reach my breaking point. I sit in the computer lab, shivering. My teeth clatter as I attempt to type up an e-mail directory for one of the groups I'm involved in. I have a private little laugh with myself—good thing I don't need to take a lunch break. I trot to the ladies' room to make some more instant coffee. I then meet up with some people from my chemistry lecture, to go over our problems for class.

I sit, all morning and a good portion of the afternoon, studying my notes for a chemistry quiz, reviewing my presentation, gulping down mug after mug of tepid coffee, shivering. I eat a lime-flavored Tootsie Roll for lunch. I run to the bathroom yet again, pee, scrub my hands in boiling hot water. I let the scalding water run over my skin, soak up the warmth as goose bumps wash over my body. I stare at my reflection in the mirror of the second-floor science building bathroom. I am staring into the face of death.

I realize my lips are completely blue. I had long since resigned myself to the perpetual bluish tinge to my nails, but now it has spread to my lips. For the first time, I see the layer of soft ducky down that covers my face and forearms. For the first time, I see the sharp jut of my cheekbones, the ghastly sunkenness that surrounds my eyes and mouth. I can no longer recognize the girl I once was, the one with full cheeks and healthy skin. I stare back into my eyes, thinking, what the hell am I *doing* to myself?

That thought marked the beginning of the end.

I walk into my chemistry class, sit down to take the quiz, and find I can only stare at the blank sheet of paper in front of me. I rummage through the contents of my brain, trying to come across any scrap of information that will help me solve the problem in front of me. There is nothing. And I am cold. The page stays blank. I hand the empty sheet to the professor, telling him I'm sorry, I'm sorry, I just can't *think*, I'm sorry. I walk out of the class, tears smudging my mascara into huge raccoon rings under my eyes. In a haze, I make my way to the counseling center for my weekly appointment.

As I neared the building, I composed myself, took a few deep, calming breaths. In, out. In. Out. There. Much better. As a reward for my near-instantaneous equanimity, I decided to allow myself a piece of candy from the selection always in front of the secretary. After carefully calculating the number of calories in a Life Saver, and doubling it, just in case, I selected a cinnamon disk from the bowl on the counter and slurped it noisily while I waited for Jeanne to make her appearance.

She followed me into her office.

"We don't have much time to play around here," she said crisply. I stared at her.

"Have you thought about leaving for a semester, taking some time off?" she asked.

"No." I continued to stare straight ahead.

Jeanne leaned forward in her overstuffed chair, resting her forearms on her thighs. "Honey, you're kidding yourself if you think you can finish out the semester."

I mulled that over for a few moments. I decided she had a point. "Yeah, well…"

She interjected before I could complete my thought. "If you pull out today you can get all of your tuition money back." It was 4:15 P.M. I gulped noisily. *You're already costing your parents too much money. You are not worth all of this. Give your parents their damned money back.* "You're clearly in need of a break, and definitely not the first person to need a semester off." That was the understatement of the year.

I stared at the toes of my running shoes, apologized again and again for being *cold*, so damn cold I couldn't see straight. I wanted, more than anything, for this hell to be over, and I began to pray for death to come soon. This must have been reflected in my face somehow, because the next words Jeanne softly said were, "You look like a ghost."

I leaned back in my chair, considered this for a moment. I sighed, then nodded.

"Good girl. Do you want me to help you with the paperwork?" Again, I nodded.

Leaving, I stood up too fast, got dizzy, nearly passed out. I clung to the arm of the chair to steady my body while my vision cleared, and fetched the forms from the adjoining office. Jeanne phoned various administrators while I filled out the stack of papers. Reason for leaving? To die. Mind your own goddamned business. Will you be returning? I don't know. What do you hope to accomplish in the interim? I don't know that, either. May we contact you? No. Go away. Leave me alone, please, and let me die in peace.

I scrawled my name in red ink at the bottom of the countless forms, making what had seemed three months ago an impossibility, very much possible. I was leaving school. Had it really come to this? Was I really too sick to continue on? Yes. I denied it then, and still partially deny it now, but that doesn't make it any less true.

I had withdrawn from all my classes at Hope. I was officially nothing more than a college drop-out.

There lurks a danger at this stage, when your eating disorder has robbed you of everything *except* your eating disorder. It's all you have, the only salvageable item to remain in the debris that was your former life. You ask yourself—is being good at something that is killing me better than being good at nothing at all?

CR

I've fallen...
I have sunk so low
I have messed up
Better I should know
So don't come round here
And tell me I told you so...

Sarah McLachlan, "Fallen"

As I trudged back to my apartment, the enormity of what I had just done hit me. I was going to have to go somewhere and gain weight, actually give in and eat something. I punctuated each step with a stomp. Damn. Damn. Damn. I had to get out of this somehow. I will *not* get fat, I vowed silently. A woman stopped me on the street, asked for the time. I mumbled something, then stopped short as her hand grasped my upper arm.

"Carrie. What the hell *happened* to you? Do you have cancer or something? You look awful." I stared at one of my classmates, my brain tripping and slipping over her name. I blinked. I hate to admit I was proud of looking like hell.

"No. It's called an eating disorder." I brushed by her, leaving her slack-jawed, staring after me. At that precise moment, I stopped worrying what anyone at Hope thought anymore. After all, I was no longer a student there.

I walked into the apartment and threw my backpack onto the floor. My roommates were cooking dinner, and they refused to meet my gaze, instead finding something intriguing on the floor. "How was your day?" they asked. "Just fine," I lied. Their gaze shifted from me to Sara. I wondered what they were talking about before I walked in.

"I've decided I'm sick of lying about how you're doing," she said loftily.

"Well, bully for you," I growled.

"I told some people today, 'Yeah, she's headed straight to the hospital. She's not even trying anymore. I give her a month until she starves herself to death.' "

I stared at her dumbly. I blinked, realized it no longer mattered.

"I withdrew from all my classes." This time it was Sara's turn to stare. "I'm leaving."

Silence.

"So, yeah. I'm moving out. Like soon. Like this weekend soon."

Silence.

"Well? *Say* something, damn you!" My voice cracked.

"Are we supposed to be *happy* for you?" Sara asked. I threw my hands into the air and stalked out of the room. "Well? Are we?"

I whirled around. "Yes. Actually, you are."

"So are you going to eat dinner now?"

"Maybe later."

"You're lying."

"So what if I am?" I shot back.

"Don't kid yourself. We both know you're not going to eat anything else today."

"Well, if you knew the answer, then why did you ask the question?" I snapped, peeved because I knew, deep down, that she was right.

The next day I ate several large plates of crow (I didn't eat anything else today! I was good! It is all going to be okay... *is* it going to be okay?) and told my professors I was leaving. No one really asked why, which I thought odd at the time. Now, I realize the lack of questions stemmed not from a dearth of curiosity but from the fact that I was visibly anorexic, practically evaporating in front of their eyes.

The remaining three days at Hope passed in a meaningless haze. I basically crashed on the couch in my apartment, too hungry to focus, too tired to move, and too depressed to give a damn. Every now and then, one of my roommates, worried out of her mind, poked me to make sure I was still breathing. I would grunt, half-heartedly, until she left me alone.

I cried a lot during those days, a rarity for me, even in that state. My life had fallen apart, simply unraveled on me. It was *not* supposed to do this. I was the valedictorian of my high school class. And now? A college drop-out. Well, that sure lifted my spirits. I considered myself a lost cause and was dumbfounded later when friends and family disagreed. I scoffed at their efforts. What the hell could there be worth saving? A ninety-pound basketcase?

My last day at Hope dawned gray and rainy, which I found very fitting. I woke up early for my weekly weigh-in at the health clinic, determined not to miss a chance at casually observing my weight as it plummeted downward. Since it no longer mattered where the scale landed, I wanted to see how low I could go, meaning I had to get every trace of food out of my system. So I swallowed half a box of laxatives to get all of that (ahem) shit out of me. I knew at that point it was just water, that the weight I had lost wasn't "real," but I vowed to only drink two glasses of liquids a day in a last-ditch effort to keep my weight headed in the downward direction.

I sat in the waiting room, glancing at brightly colored brochures proclaiming that you, too, could get hepatitis B, that sex could wait, and that the time to get a meningitis vaccine was *now*. I noted absently the multicultural crowd of students in the brochure that was clearly not reflective of the exclusively WASP environment of Hope and the rest of small-town America. I occupied myself by studying the other students in the waiting room, whose furtive glances matched mine. I decided they were probably getting flu shots, whereas I would be stripped down, given a paper gown, and rather unceremoniously plunked down on a scale. Before I went in, I asked to use the bathroom (damn laxatives). Afterward, I wallowed in the feeling of emptiness that follows a laxative purge. *There is nothing inside of me.* No food. No feelings. Nothing. My head began to spin as I realized I had found nirvana in a box of extra-strength Ex-Lax.

All decked out in a paper gown, I sat on the examining table, shivering, waiting. With a gentle rap, the door opened and the nurse walked in. "I heard what's happened," she said quietly. "Jeanne told me. I think you made the right decision." I nodded, floored at this display of gentleness and compassion, blinking back the few tears that hadn't yet frozen up inside me. "Now I guess it really won't matter whether we weigh you or not." The nurse laughed awkwardly at her little joke. I managed a sad smile.

"I guess not." I closed my eyes and hunched my shoulders forward, trying to collapse inward upon myself and calm the raging river of pain inside.

"Do you still want me to get your weight?"

I shrugged. "You may as well. I'm already here. Besides," I lied, "the treatment centers need to know when they admit you."

As I hopped on the scale, a thrill of excitement ran down my spine. How much weight had I lost in the past week? My heart pounded, the adrenaline rush almost unbearable. I closed my eyes in preparation for the big moment.

"Dear God." I gingerly opened one eyelid at the nurse's hoarse whisper. "Could you really have managed to lose that much weight in only a week?"

I looked at the scale. Eighty-nine pounds. Was I really that skinny? Had I finally done it? Could I now call myself a respectable anorexic? I stifled a scream of excitement—my weight was actually in the *eighties*! The only thing left to do now was keep going. Looking back, I realize they should have called 911 and hauled my sorry ass to the hospital without hesitation. I had lost approximately ten pounds in one week, and my heart pumped a piddly forty-four times per minute. At forty beats per minute, I would later learn, you die.

The nurse let me change back into my street clothes, then came in to prep me for what life in an eating disorder treatment facility was like. After we discussed the advantages of a dorm-like setting and the joy of having several months to work on myself, she rose to leave. "Can I give you a hug?" she asked, stepping forward and wrapping her arms around my shoulders. "Sure," I mumbled, embarrassed at this sudden show of affection, and fearful she would feel the outline of my sports bra and figure out that I was headed to the gym. I laughed bitterly to myself. What could they do anyway—kick me out of school?

That afternoon, I gave a presentation for the biology department about the benefits of obtaining an off-campus internship, speaking about my time at the CDC. I have hazy memories of gushing on and on about how much I had enjoyed my time in Atlanta, how wonderful the experience had been for me. I remember suddenly seeing my chemistry professor standing in the back of the room. I could not bring myself to meet his sad gaze. As he walked out of the lecture hall, I suddenly realized that not everyone was envious of my emaciation. I know it sounds completely ridiculous, but up until that point, I never understood that, to most people, I was not a girl to emulate, I was a girl to pity. I couldn't help but think that this time last year, I was packing to go to Scotland. This time last year, I was hopeful and healthy and *happy*. How far I had fallen, and how fast. Yet all I could do was stand there helpless, wondering when I would finally strike rock bottom.

My friends took me out for coffee on Friday night, for a combination bon voyage and good luck party. The party included Sara and our two other roommates, Liz and Dana, as well as my good friend from the *Anchor*, Julie. The conversation centered around classes, and I silently observed my little circle of friends, uncomfortably aware that their normal college lives *should* have been mine, too. How I should have been bitching about papers and lab reports, also. But I wasn't. I was worrying about the cherry tomato I had eaten for lunch and wondering how to squirm my way out of ordering a drink with calories in it.

Sara spent the evening attempting to garner sympathy from the rest of the group because she had a best friend (me) who was deathly ill, possibly dying, and Lord only knew if she would get well. This did not go over very well with the rest of the group, in particular me. I sat, outraged but mute, trying to figure out how someone could be worse off than me. After all, Sara wasn't leaving school, leaving home, holding the shards of her former life. Sara wasn't going to have to figure out how to reconstruct her very being right from scratch. Even on the drive home, I would get a word or two out about how I was feeling, only to have Sara interject something about how horrible her life was and how I should be a little more understanding.

Maybe I was being a little selfish, not letting her express her frustrations about watching her closest friend try to kill herself. I'll admit it. But I simply couldn't handle it. I couldn't deal with my own problems, and I was clearly in no shape to take on someone else's. I rebuffed any forgiving actions on Sara's behalf, still too pissed off to trust myself to speak. I wanted to fling the stuffed animal she had left on my pillow to the ground, and tell her that real friends didn't blab to the entire campus that their roommates had eating disorders. But I didn't say anything. I know now what her actions were trying to say— Don't forget about me in all this mess. Please don't forget about me. I'm hurting, too.

Julie and I took a long walk on that crisp fall evening long after everyone had returned to their rooms. We chatted simultaneously about trivialities and Life's Big Questions. That stroll through the deserted streets of Holland softened something in my soul, made me believe I had a chance to get my life back together and move on. I scuffed my shoes as we walked, my mind a million miles away, but absorbing every speck of warmth and unconditional love that emanated from the person next to me. I positively ate it up. The girl who wouldn't, couldn't, eat anything, could still, at the very least, take in love and hope.

Saturday dawned bright and early as my parents arrived to move me out of my apartment. I felt like I was watching a movie of my life. Those aren't *really* my pots and pans jammed into that box. That isn't *my* ivy plant cradled in half a roll of paper towels. My parents did most of the packing. I laid in a heap on the couch, curled up in the fetal position, crying softly. No one bothered to disturb me.

Farewells were brief and awkward. I gave each of my roommates a stiff hug, then turned to face Sara. Dear God, what to say. I dissolved into tears, extending my hand, gently stroking her cheek. I whispered, "I'm sorry, so sorry, it'll all be okay, I promise, I'm sorry." She said nothing in return. She didn't have to. We took turns at the bathroom sink washing away the mascara rings our tears had painted beneath our eyes.

When the last box had been taped shut and the last load toted to the car, I took stock of the now almost ghostly apartment. I signed various forms, certifying that everything was in the same condition as when I moved in only two weeks before. This whole process twisted my lips in a sad, sardonic smile—I hadn't had time to do much damage. As we waited for the elevator to arrive, I realized that this was it, that I would never come back to school, at least not in the way I had anticipated. Although I could physically return to Hope College, my spirit had long since fled.

I spent most of the drive home tossing and turning in a fitful doze. I woke briefly for a pit stop while my dad refueled the car. I was stretching my legs in a stroll around the gas pump when my mom tugged at the waist of my jeans. "What pants are these?" she asked me. "They look huge."

"My new ones." I shrugged. "Why?"

"They're *huge*," she repeated. "Could you really have lost that much weight in only two weeks?"

"Guess so." I hiked my pants back up around my waist and wrapped my arms around my middle. I gently rubbed the protruding edges of the back of my pelvis. "After all," I added with a bitter laugh, "I didn't leave Hope because I was doing *well*, now, did I?"

"I guess not."

I arrived home in a gray haze of misery and despair, and slowly began making arrangements to enter treatment at the Renfrew Center. The first time, it had been almost impulsive. I went into treatment because my therapist had told me to go. End of story. I didn't particularly care about getting better or making any significant changes in my behavior. I knew this time was different—I had one choice left—get better or die. And for the several weeks I spent at my parents' house before treatment, that choice paralyzed me. I stood several times in front of the medicine cabinet, staring at the amazing array of painkillers in front of me, knowing I could end all my sorrow and suffering in one easy shot.

Hours melted into days, days into weeks. During this pre-treatment time, I kept meticulous track of everything I ate in a battered old notebook. As I reviewed my notes at the end of the day, I grew horrified at the sheer volume of food I was eating. One day, I remember I ate a light yogurt (one hundred calories) and a small apple (eighty calories). To me, this was a feast. Bottles of Diet Snapple I had bought in the summer sat untouched in the fridge because they weighed in at a whopping twenty-five calories each. The amount of food I was consuming, or rather *not* consuming, did not have enough bulk to, shall we say, keep me regular. Despairing of ever taking a dump again, I swallowed the remainder of the box of laxatives I had smuggled home from Hope. Since there was nothing left in my system to dump, I sat on the toilet and shit water, the sheer futility of my actions escaping my starved brain.

And then, one bright, sunny Tuesday morning in mid-September, everything changed.

I woke up and flipped on the TV as the second Twin Tower came crashing down, wondering what kind of movie I was watching. My dad called home from work, asking, "Are you following this? What the hell is *happening* out there?" I wept, out of anger, frustration, and grief. How many people had just lost their lives, and how many more would follow? I was consumed, too, by the thought of the five celery sticks I had munched as I sat in front of the TV, entranced by the unfolding events. I realized I was terrorized more by what the stalks might do to my body than by the hijacked airplanes. I knew this was wrong, that I should not be worrying about celery when people were dying. I thought about how I would feel if I were in one of those buildings, knowing how much time I had wasted obsessing over food and weight, and knowing that there was still so much left I wanted to do.

A few days later, I went to my mother's doctor for a checkup, as required by Renfrew before they would admit me (my own doctor was stuck overseas in the aftermath of September 11). I went in and they sat me down, wrapped the blood pressure cuff around my arm. It was too big. I found this hysterically funny—my body disappearing before my very eyes. The nurse brought in the kid-sized cuff from the pediatrician's office down the hall, hooked it up to her stethoscope, and tried to get a reading. And tried again. And again. And again. *She couldn't get my blood pressure.* Five different nurses rotated through the examining room, each of them making an attempt. No luck. I shifted uncomfortably in the chair—which, though stuffed, still hurt my bones—and all of them shook their heads in confusion. "We know you have a BP because you're still living," one of them commented to me. I was so proud of this, of successfully walking the tightrope between life and death, I almost burst. The nurses gathered in a hushed conference, occasionally stealing a glance at me. They eventually had me lay on the examining table, elevating my feet over my head. The sphygmomanometer barely registered at 80/50. It was no wonder, then, that I nearly passed out each time I stood up.

I also had to have an EKG, which was another adventure into the Land of the Living Dead. Once again, they hooked me up, and once again, they couldn't get a reading. They changed electrodes and tried again. Nothing. By this time, I had become something of a curiosity in the doctor's office, the Mysterious Case of the Girl Who Should Be Dead But Wasn't. The nurses messed around with the electrodes once again, and this time, the EKG machine picked up a signal—my heart fluttered, half-useless in my chest, almost too weak to keep on pumping. Because it wasn't grossly uneven, just way too slow and ungodly weak, no one said a word to me about the perilous state of my health. Oddly, my lab results came back perfectly normal, which shocked and disappointed me (I measured my success at anorexia in direct relation to my crumbling physical health). There was no way for anyone to have known that my heart didn't spurt my blood into the blood collection tube like it should have. Instead, it had sort of meandered in on its own accord, my heart too tired to give it the oomph it needed. And so, I was, hilariously, given a clean bill of health and sent on my way.

That night, after my shower, I stared at my reflection in the full-length bathroom mirror. I examined my shrunken frame, not out of an ooh-I'm-so-skinny feeling, but because I finally wanted to see the mastery of my body. My body was a thing outside of me, so what did it matter if I killed it? Soon, my body would be gone completely, and I prayed for God to take it from me. I wanted to seize my body and fling it away from me, like the disgusting, ugly, worthless thing that it really was. I grabbed what was left of my butt, gave it a jiggle. How much more weight would I have to lose before this, too, was gone? How much more until I disappeared entirely? I saw death as the ultimate victory—in death, my mind would have finally won out over my pitiful, weak body.

The next day, I reluctantly accompanied my parents to an eating disorder support group meeting at Beaumont Hospital, staring at my feet the entire time, terrified that I would be the fattest one there. I half-listened to the doctor as he spoke, my mind swirling instead with thoughts of what was to become of me. Though I tried to pass it off as just being directly in his line of sight, I soon realized he was speaking directly to me. "People with eating disorders are some of the brightest and best people out there," he said. "We need them back." His gaze met mine. I shifted uncomfortably in my chair.

"He's looking right at me," I hissed to my mother. "How does he know I'm anorexic? How does he know?"

"Honey," she whispered gently, "I can count each and every bone in your neck. Trust me. People can tell just by looking at you." I mulled that thought over for the rest of the evening, still baffled. My mother told me later that she was half tempted to take me down to the emergency room and simply leave me there. "I held my breath," she said. "I just held my breath and prayed to God you wouldn't die before you got help."

Help came in the nick of time. The night before I left for Renfrew, I parted the sea of clothing on my bed and threw myself into the comforter. As I lay there in the dark, I took my pulse, waiting as it slowed and dragged me off into sleep. I had strict instructions from the nurse who managed my medications to haul myself to the emergency room if my pulse ever fell below sixty. My exhausted heart fluttered sixty-two… fifty-five… fifty-one… forty-nine… forty-four. I knew I was in serious danger, but I felt so peaceful as I laid there, I decided that it wouldn't be bad to die now. As I thought of this, I tried to picture my family and Sara at my funeral. I thought of my lunch of baby carrots, the half-cup of plain Cheerios I had measured out for my dinner tomorrow, and realized how pathetic my life had become.

CR

Because I could not stop for Death
He kindly stopped for me—
The carriage held but just ourselves
And Immortality.

Emily Dickinson, "Because I could not stop for Death"

The next day, I awoke all revved up for what I knew would be my last day of restricting. I also woke up too late to devote a full hour to my morning yogurt ritual, so I opted out of breakfast. My mom packed a carton for me anyway in the vain hope I would eat it. I politely sat it next to me in the backseat of the car and tried to read. But my brain kept escaping the pages in front of me and drifting back to the yogurt.

I eventually slouched down in my seat, ripped the foil top off, and played with its contents with my spoon. After stirring for forty-five minutes, I took a few half-hearted licks, then put the whole thing down.

My parents stopped for lunch at Wendy's. I ordered a diet soda and sat down at the table with my baggie of baby carrots. "Are you sure you don't want anything?" my mom asked.

"I'm sure," I crunched contentedly, filling up the empty hole in my middle with giant slurps of soda. I watched my parents eat, the weaklings, staring at their double bacon cheeseburgers with a revulsion tinged with desire, mouth watering at the feast in front of me. I justified my handful of carrots, more than I ever would have eaten on my own, as merely a token gift to my parents. I quietly washed my saliva down with another swig of diet cola. I sat back and watched the other people in Wendy's eat their burgers and fries, enjoying the sight of so many weaklings who broke down and caved in to their appetites. Me? I felt the need of hunger press hard against my middle, felt myself embrace it, then felt myself rise above it, ethereal and free from all wants and desires.

I drifted off to sleep back in the car, waking only briefly for a pit stop on the Pennsylvania turnpike. Though we were in the midst of an Indian summer, I shivered in a long-sleeved T-shirt and jacket. The rest stop where we parked had a Cinnabon kiosk that smelled of sweet heaven. I stood in front of it, enamored, entranced by the wonderful aroma of warm, sticky cinnamon. The next time I pass this, I realized, I may actually *eat* here. I shuddered, horrified at my probable descent into gluttony. For now, though, I was still in control. For now, I was safe. My parents made a half-hearted suggestion of getting a snack for the rest of the car ride. I laughed bitterly. What? Me, eat? I instead ordered a black coffee, garnering a long look from the girl behind the counter. Her eyes followed my skeletal figure as I walked over to add sweetener to my drink. I thought she was just jealous. Now I know she was waiting for me to fall over dead.

In the rest stop bathroom, I emptied my bladder of the two-liter of Diet Coke I had drank that afternoon in the car. I stood up, looked down, checked the plane of my stomach. Completely flat, and maybe (gasp!) concave, a C-shaped curve emphasized by my blue panties. I gave a satisfied nod and zipped up my jeans. Good girl. Keep it up. And enjoy it while it lasts.

We decided to press on through to Philadelphia and not stop for dinner until late, a decision that sat just fine with me. I lay in the backseat, idly watching the sunset, my brain too overwhelmed to read. I silently raged at those people who didn't have their disorders "taken" from them as was happening to me. I thought of the sleek swimsuit models—no one was breathing down their necks to get them to eat or gain weight.

As I watched the clouds drift by the car window, I finally understood the magnitude of what had happened to me. My weight had dwindled to eighty-five pounds (I had insisted, much to my mother's dismay, on checking the night before), a near anorexic record weight loss of fifty pounds in six months, and I had the skeletal look of a concentration camp victim, not the sleek lines of a fashion model. Here I was, over five hundred miles from home, going God only knows where, leaving my home and my friends. As it stood then, I was never going to make it to my college graduation. And why? For what? All because I didn't like the size of my jeans? How ridiculous was that? The fury built interminably, and I knew my top would blow any second. After checking into the hotel, we went out to a restaurant for a late dinner. I flipped through a brightly colored Ruby Tuesday menu while my parents took turns using the bathroom. Overwhelmed by the photos of food in front of me, I did the one and only thing I could.

I binged.

I knew that the next day I would have to eat anyway, so I figured what the hell. My mom asked me later why I didn't start to eat the second I knew I would be entering treatment, and the answer was simply that I couldn't. I literally could not eat, could not pick up the damned fork and do the seemingly easy task in front of me. It's hard to explain, really, being so hungry that you think you are going to claw your way out of your skull, and yet being completely incapable of doing anything about it. But when the dam breaks, it breaks, and that night I went all-out as the water rushed over the dykes with a giant roar.

While my parents ordered entrees, I opted for fried mozzarella sticks and a chocolate sundae. Only the greasiest for me. I garnered a look of outright disgust from our waitress, as she tried to understand how such a skinny person could eat like this. I inhaled the food in front of me, hardly pausing between bites. A few bites into the sundae, however, I realized I was stuffed, but I was so malnourished that I kept right on eating.[13] Eventually, though, my stomach felt like it was going

---

[13] During anorexia, the stomach actually shrinks down to the size of a plum, and food takes much longer to digest, a phenomenon known as delayed gastric emptying. In my third hospitalization, I found I needed medication to temporarily counteract this until my digestive system returned to normal.

to burst. I foolishly believed I had conquered my eating disorder in an evening. I thought I was in the clear. I only had to gain about five or ten pounds, get my weight back into the nineties, and my life would return to normal. Simple as that. Little did I know my fight had only just begun. I still had so much to learn.

Twenty minutes after I had finished eating, I bent over to tie my shoe, and my dinner tried to come rushing back up. My food was literally sitting in my stomach, undigested, because my body had forgotten how to digest anything more complex than vegetables and mustard. With great effort, I managed to keep it down, though I was sorely tempted to make my way to the bathroom and empty everything into the toilet. I thought fleetingly of the rest of the laxatives I had taken just before I left, how much they would have come in handy now. I silently recriminated myself for not buying more, even if I wouldn't get to keep them once I entered Renfrew. Truth be told, I was too afraid someone would see me buying them. Back in the hotel, I jumped in the shower, looking down at my now-bloated stomach. I thought back to earlier that afternoon at the rest stop. How was I going to undo this one? Couldn't I have waited just one more day? Pig. I curled up in bed and flipped through the TV channels, thinking vaguely about writing in my journal. I decided against it, decided I didn't want the headline "Anorexic Eats Sundae" recorded permanently. My brain, finally sated enough to think of something besides food, soared, skipped, and jumped, and finally became still, my sleep deep and dreamless.

> *'Cause when you live in the world,*
> *well, it gets into who you thought you'd be,*
> *and now I laugh at how the world changed me.*
> *I think life chose me—after all.*

Dar Williams, "After All"

When I arrived at Renfrew bright and early the next morning, I was startled by the fact that no one, staff or resident, bothered to ask me what particular problem had brought me to a Philadelphia psychiatric facility. I mean, they specialized in eating disorders, so there had to be something wrong with how I ate, but I had no idea how they could determine whether I was anorexic or bulimic. I didn't know that even an idiot could see, in my emaciated silhouette, the vestiges of a tumultuous battle with anorexia that had consumed my flesh almost in its entirety.

I checked into Renfrew not knowing how much of a fight I had before me.

If I have inside me the stuff to make cocoons—maybe the stuff of butterflies is there too.

Trina Paulus, *Hope for the Flowers*

Chapter Seven: Hope for the Flowers
The Renfrew Center, Philadelphia, Pennsylvania, Fall 2001

I grabbed the pen they gave me to officially sign myself in, and wrote my name perfectly on the line. I was given the ubiquitous purple folder with all of the rules and regulations of the Renfrew Center, including general Renfrew policy, which I scanned and consequently forgot, as well as the list of meal plans, food options, and an explanation of Mealtime Support Therapy (MST), which I pored over every night and eventually committed to memory.

First, I was plunked down on a scale in the classic blue paper gown. Drawings and inspirational posters littered the oversized closet they weighed us in each morning, with sayings like "You are more than a number!" I chose to get on the scale backwards, hoping that this would get me the hell out of there a little sooner. They took me back into an examination room to get my blood pressure and pulse, first sitting, then standing.

"Can you get a reading?" asked one nurse to another. "I can't hear anything," she said, as she removed the stethoscope from the crook of my elbow. Several other nurses gathered around as they took turns, each trying to solve the Mystery of the Silent Sphygmomanometer. "Well, you're standing there, so we know you *have* a blood pressure," someone joked. I laughed weakly at the now-familiar joke, wondering if they would turn me away. What would I tell my parents—thanks for the trip, but I was too sick for treatment?

I know someone, at some point, had to have been able to measure *something* resembling a blood pressure because I was, indeed, admitted to Renfrew at that time. I was given a large glass of fluorescent lemon-lime Gatorade to drink, to "balance my electrolytes"[14] and help raise my blood pressure out of the basement. I held the Styrofoam cup with both hands, and took a tentative sip of the neon green liquid. Blech—tasted like flat Mountain Dew. I didn't really like the carbonated version, let alone this shit. I debated pouring the Gatorade into a nearby shrub, realized there were too many people watching, and instead plugged my nose and finished the drink in one long glug.

Soon enough, lunchtime had arrived. To this day, I have no idea what my parents did while I learned my way around the Renfrew dining room. Rules abounded, which I sort of expected, though I still saw plenty of cheating. I found the tray with my name on it, inspected the contents. One veggie burger with cheese. One bun. One apple. One pack of carrot and celery sticks (oh, yum!). I threw the bun in the toaster, removed the cellophane from the little plate with the veggie burger and cheese. I imagined the burger smiling happily up at me, though its innate goodness was concealed by an evil coating of American cheese, the demonic Fat Monster. As I started to peel the layer of plastic cheese off the burger, the girl sitting next to me whispered, "It's okay. The cheese is low fat." Oh. Well, then. I still wanted to yank the cheese off, but I didn't want to be considered completely neurotic, so I left the cheese in place. I stared at the food, hoping it wouldn't attack me.

The beginning of mealtime is ritualistic at any eating disorder treatment center, largely due to the sheer number of rules in place. No jackets or baggy sweatshirts. Bags must be checked at the door. One napkin per meal (though you were allowed a replacement if you turned in the first one). Before you could start eating, a counselor had to make sure what you had selected and what you had on your tray actually matched. No getting up and walking around during meals. No scrutinizing your menu was allowed, neither was any discussion of weight, calories, specific meal plans or clothing sizes. One cup of coffee or tea unless you finished everything on your tray, then you were permitted a

---

[14] Though purging, whether through self-induced vomiting or laxative/diuretic abuse, tends to disturb electrolyte levels much more radically, starvation also disrupts sodium and potassium levels, leading to heart attacks and, in some instances, death.

second. Only once you had continually finished all of your meals could you use the microwave—quite a treat considering most of the food was served tepid at best. Eagle-eyed counselors kept watch over the lot of us while we painstakingly dissected our food trays, noting any of our "food rituals" (more on these later). Between the food rituals we brought with us and all of the rules imposed by staff, it was a wonder we got anything eaten at all.

As much as we all bitched about having to follow these rules, we:
a) needed them,
b) soon began to look forward to them.

After all, most of our existence revolved around food rituals. We were, quite simply, replacing old ones with new ones. And let me tell you, I saw some pretty interesting phobias. I had, up until that point, thought that my little world of food idiosyncrasies was pretty bizarre, which, to the non-eating disordered population, they were. But I slowly began to see that eating really slowly and cutting everything up into itsy bitsy pieces was only the tip of the iceberg. Some rituals were obvious, like covering everything on the tray with a thick layer of salt or sweetener. Others were much more subtle—chewing a certain number of times or daintily curling one's lips back away from the tines of the fork. I, on the other hand, dutifully arranged the food on my tray in alphabetical order, then rearranged it so I would eat the foods with the least calories first. Then I just stared at my plate with a look that said, what am I supposed to do with all this food?

I began to eat my first real meal in months starting with the carrots and celery sticks, figuring there wasn't much harm in those. My heart pounded as I moved on to the veggie burger. I pecked at it like a little bird, taking one tiny bite, then another, then another. When the first half had been pecked off, I put the remaining part of the burger down and moved on to my apple. I personally like to get down and dirty with my pieces of fruit, seeing no real need to cut them into bite-sized bits. But here, slicing and dicing was the fashion, so once again I capitulated.

I nibbled my way through lunch and, for some odd reason, finished everything. I figured I would be asked to drink a supplement of Ensure if I didn't finish, so I somehow felt I had permission to eat. Eating disorders are positively notorious for recidivism (though each treatment center will try to wow you with statistics indicating that its method works otherwise), and the reason I think so many people can't yank themselves out of treatment is because they feel they're "allowed" to eat at the treatment center (or to not purge or not exercise manically). Treatment becomes a safe haven, and some people make a home of it. And this is how anorexics get sucked into repeatedly seeking treatment, because they've found the one place where they feel justified to pick up their forks and shovel food into their mouths.

After lunch, the next memory I have is of a counselor doing the obligatory search of my belongings. This time, I didn't have any illicit laxatives or packets of artificial sweetener, so I paid very little attention to what the girl was saying. ("Are you listening, Carrie?" "Huh? What did you say?" "I didn't think so.") I hauled my trunkful of belongings, the suitcases and crates of books weighing more than I did at this point, into the room directly across from the nurses' station. This special room, replete with a full wall of windows so staff could observe our every move, was typically reserved for those patients in need of bed rest. I was not aware that my condition, at that moment in time, warranted such treatment, nor would it dawn on me during my treatment there. I knew I had barely dodged the bullet, weighing in only a pound or two above the cutoff for placement on bedrest, and I knew the extra weight was from the previous night's binge. I hadn't breathed a word about it to anyone at Renfrew (nor would I, at any point during my stay), and I'm sure they credited my magical and mysterious five-pound weight gain to "water loading" and other such tricks, not to the actual presence of food in my system. Eventually, of course, they let me off the hook, but until then I took up residence in the "fish bowl" front room.

As I unpacked, my parents hovered nervously at the door. I don't blame them for being apprehensive. Here they were, entrusting their daughter's fragile life to complete strangers. I cannot imagine the difficulty of having to admit that you had somehow failed as a parent and needed outside help to save your child. "You looked so frail," my mom said later. "I watched you standing there and I just waited for you to fall over." My parents stayed as long as they could, but eventually they had to leave if they were to make it to my grandmother's house at a decent hour. The three of us were emotional basketcases, my mom and I crying openly. One of the counselors told me it was afternoon snacktime and steered me towards the dining room. Great. Food. Just what I wanted to do—eat. I protested that snacktime was ridiculous for grown women, and we were grown women, weren't we? Snacks were for little kids. I was, however, shuttled in to the dining room. The counselor handed me a little folder with my name on the front, and I opened it, stared at the little numbers in the boxes marked "fats," "grains," "proteins," and so on.

Renfrew muffin (whatever the hell *that* was)—1 fat, 1 grain
Milk—1 protein

My stomach didn't seem large enough to hold all of that food.

Snacks were run a little differently than meals. Residents were expected to pick out their own snacks from the variety of foods considered "appropriate" for snacktime. The process was supposed to empower us to make our own food selections. I didn't personally see the point of this, though I did like the fact that I got to pick the flavor of yogurt and NutriGrain bars I frequently selected. We were allotted precisely half an hour to complete our snacks, and those of us that didn't finish were asked to drink a supplement.

Three-oh-five. I make my selection, gingerly picking a pecan muffin out of the basket and a carton of milk (dark green writing, definitely *not* skim) out of the refrigerator. I pour myself a glass of water to wash it all down, then move on to the carafe of coffee.

Three-ten. I break my muffin into two neat, even halves, then go about shredding it as I try to pick out all of the pecans. I figure, what the hell, this is still my first day, and go about making little pecan piles on my napkin. I take quick, nervous sips of black coffee between mini-bites of muffin. I am aware that I am being watched by staff, but I have resigned myself to being a patient, some sort of specimen preserved in formaldehyde. After I have finished dissecting my muffin, leaving an incredible pile of crumbs on my tray, I move on to my milk. I examine the carton, scrutinizing every inch of cardboard. In big, bold, green letters, the carton reads, "2% Reduced Fat Milk." Firstly, I only drink skim. Secondly, didn't the nutritionist here *know* that 2% is *not* low-fat milk? If we have to drink this, we certainly should be able to mark off one of our fats. I shudder at the thought of all those little droplets of milkfat racing for my thighs, where they will be preserved, safe and sound, for all eternity. What the hell is *up* with this place? No skim milk, no aspartame-laced yogurts, no diet soda, nothing. What am I supposed to *eat* while I'm here? I was half-afraid my system would go into chemical shock after going for so long with all of that aspartame leeching out from my stomach and intestines.

Three-twenty. I pry the carton open and stuff a straw inside. I take one mini-sip, then another, look down at my hips to make sure they haven't gotten bigger. I can't be sure. Panic washes over me, and I begin to lose my grip, drowning in a sea of thoughts and worries. So much for the milk. What to do with myself now? I absently blow little milk bubbles into the carton with the straw, and watch the other residents finish their snacks. After staff checks to make sure they have indeed finished their snacks—a fairly thorough process: shake out the napkins, rattle the cartons of milk and juice, inspect the neat little hidey-hole underneath the plates—the women begin to stand up and throw away their cellophane wrappers and napkins, pour themselves a second cup of coffee, and chat with their neighbors.

The girl who had clued me in to the low-fat cheese is nervously pecking at her concoction of yogurt, granola, and apples, sparrow-like in her motions. She has just started in on her snack after an elaborate series of preparations, and I am aware of what this implies. Those who take longest to finish at mealtimes are usually the ones with the most phobias and rituals regarding food. This means staff keeps a closer eye on you than anyone else, and only serves to make you more determined to rebel, to throw a stake in their wheels. That you're only hindering your own recovery never occurs to you at the time. I absently consider all of this while I nibble on a piece of pecan.

Three-twenty-five. I pick at some more muffin crumbs from my pile of nuts. I swirl the milk around in the carton. I stare at the endless snacks stretched out in front of me, the vista spreading out from horizon to horizon. I realize it's a lost cause. Tears flood my eyes, and slip softly, quietly down my face and onto the napkin in my lap. One of the counselors, a gruff middle-aged woman who frankly scares the hell out of me, comes over to me, rummages through my crumb-strewn tray. She stares suspiciously at the pile of muffin crumbs, gives the mostly full milk carton a little shake.

"How much do you think she's eaten?" she says, calling another counselor to come over. "Two out of four, or only one?"

The second counselor stares at the dissected muffin. "One out of four." Gee, thanks, just talk about me like I'm not here. That is one surefire way to make people feel better.

Thankfully, because it is my first day, I am not asked to drink a supplement of Ensure or Deliver (a meal-replacement drink like Ensure, only it tastes worse and packs more of a calorie-punch) though I don't think I would have drunk it anyway. At that point, I don't think I would have even touched a can of Slim-Fast.

The only thing I could do was sit there and cry.

I know I must have left the dining hall at some point, though I have no memory of putting my tray away or walking back to my fish-bowl room. My roommate, who was on full bedrest at the time and thus not allowed to venture into the dining hall, asked me how snack was and I told her, "Awful, just awful," and didn't elaborate. She didn't pry—she understood all too well.

I explored the grounds of Renfrew during free time and learned, much to my dismay, that I was one of only about five women there who didn't smoke. Everyone else gathered in groups, little clusters of smoke and fluttering ash, talking and laughing, sometimes loudly, mostly quietly. Women lit cigarette after cigarette, chain-smoking and talking and talking and talking. I tried to join in some of their conversations, sitting on the front steps of the residence hall with everyone else, but I felt too much of a chasm between us.

Boys and school were no longer a part of my life. Instead, I sat in the gazebo on a wooden bench that dug into the bruises at the base of my spine, staring idly at the trees, letting the late afternoon sun bathe my pale skin. I made a pilgrimage to this bench almost daily to monitor my weight gain and found that, after a while, it wasn't so uncomfortable. This terrified me. To this day, I refuse to sit on anything but the most uncomfortable chairs and benches, so that my bones feel like they protrude more than they actually do.

One of the hallmarks of the Renfrew Center, promoted in all of its nice, shiny pamphlets, is its Mealtime Support Therapy (MST). MST was meant to be run by a counselor immediately after mealtimes, and was an opportunity to discuss topics that were otherwise forbidden at the dinner table. We were supposed to process the feelings that were evoked by our food. Basically, it was an opportunity for us to sit around and bitch for half an hour about how the food sucked and how unfair our meal plans were and how much weight we knew we'd gained in the past hour. I found it remarkably therapeutic. It helped me to know that I wasn't the only one who felt like she was the size of a water buffalo. It was also a rather effective way to keep everyone's head out of the toilet bowl.

During MST, as in all of our groups at Renfrew, we spoke in assertive "I Feel" statements ("When I look at your tray, I feel jealous because you have less to eat than me."). I wanted to yell that "I feel like a cow is how I feel!" although I was continuously reminded that "fat" was not a feeling. "How are you *really* feeling right now?" staff would ask me. "I don't *know*," I would say, shrugging my shoulders. And I honestly didn't. I'd been keeping all of my emotions submerged in the raging sea of anorexia for so long that I no longer even knew the difference between "happy" and "sad."

All in all, I kind of liked MST, especially as they began to up the ante on my food intake. Sharing your feelings is definitely better than keeping them to yourself. One of the cornerstones of MST is, of all things, stones. There was a big pile of them in the middle of the room, and in order to speak, we had to take a stone. We were told that it symbolically demonstrated our willingness to speak up and take a risk. I found them to be rather fun to fidget with while I was trying to think of something to say that wouldn't make me look callous or uncaring (It's only cottage cheese—get *over* it!) or like the weight-obsessed freak that I was.

The most interesting part about MST was discovering how alike everyone's feelings were. My time at Rogers had only served to create a chasm between the different diagnoses of anorexia, bulimia, and the potluck of everything else. I thought that if the people at Renfrew (a center specializing in only eating disorders) had any sense, they would separate us based on diagnosis and go from there. I was wrong. An eating disorder is a way of using food to deal with your feelings. So it doesn't matter whether you eat a ton, you eat a ton and then throw it up, or you perpetually nibble at a wilted leaf of lettuce. I traded tales of the stunts I had pulled in hiding and getting rid of food with one woman in particular, who had pulled stunts just as elaborate to obtain and hide binge food.

"It's a good thing we didn't know each other then—we would have created one hell of a smuggling operation," I joked.

I quickly began to realize how alike the eating disordered population really was. Though our oversized purses were used for opposite purposes, we both shrouded our behaviors in secrecy and stealth. Even though we both knew our behaviors were irrational, we nonetheless felt compelled to do them. Shining the light on our behaviors was a very healing experience, because it removed the cloak of guilt and shame in which our actions were hidden.

As much as mealtime was charged with negative emotions, it was also filled with the occasional triumph. What had remained a tantamount secret for everyone struggling with an eating disorder, gradually, gently, eased its way out of the closet. It started as a small whisper into the night, then a hushed admission during MST, then a plaintive cry in the dining hall: we were hungry. For food, to be sure, but also for companionship, for freedom, for life. To many of us, indeed, most of us, this proclamation represented nothing less than our own personal revolution—we had been "not hungry" for so long that the words just seemed to pop out of our mouths even when we were thinking and feeling the direct opposite.

Meals turned into days turned into weeks turned into one month, then two. As I got used to eating again, my body slowly adjusted. I had finally surrendered to the system, stopped fighting every bite of food I put into my mouth. I don't particularly know why I did this, though I think it was largely because I grew weary of the constant struggle to starve. I had also become acutely, painfully aware that everyone else I knew was getting on with their lives, while I was mired in a dreadfully boring, yet all-encompassing titanic battle of To Eat or Not To Eat. While Sara and the rest of my chemistry-major friends were titrating acids in lab, I was smearing fingerpaints around on posterboard. I missed my old life, and the only way to find my way back was to close my eyes, grit my teeth, and gain the weight. I didn't have to like it. I just had to do it.

And so, time passed. Fall was glorious that year—the air tasted of apples, and the tree-lined Pennsylvania hills surrounding Renfrew exploded into color. The leaves seemed to be in a contest to see who could produce the most flamboyant shade of red, orange, or yellow. I studied the way the azure sky, dappled with dollops of Cool Whip clouds, contrasted against the green grass and Technicolor foliage. Colors seemed more intense, somehow, through my hope-tinted glasses, the brightness of oils and tempuras on canvas instead of faded watercolors on notebook paper.

Until, of course, I freaked.

I was becoming, God forbid, *normal*, and I didn't quite know how to deal with it. For so long, I had related to the world as a sick person that health seemed somehow foreign, unnatural. My emaciation had made me special, turned heads on the street and caused people to look twice. Now it was all gone and I just felt so ordinary, so plain. A peahen to the peacock, you might say. Also at this point, the real world began to butt in on the little Renfrew bubble I was living in. In a utopian paradise like Renfrew, little annoyances didn't arise, or if they did, they were like a little itch you could scratch. I had an itch on the one square inch of my back that I couldn't reach no matter how hard I twisted and squirmed...

My parents and I had started bickering about follow-up care, about what they wanted, what I wanted, what was practical. It was a fairly asinine argument, as far as arguments go. The stupidest thing was that we all basically agreed with one another. I remember the phone call, which rapidly degraded into a screaming match between my father and me. We hurled obscenities back and forth at each other for almost an hour while my mother stayed silent on the other extension, probably thinking it was good there were five hundred miles between us. I stormed back to my room, sobbing hysterically, shrieking to my roommate that my parents had ruined everything, they were going to steal my town of Perfect away from me and leave me in the real world.

We had, as a family, agreed that I should step down to a partial hospitalization (day) program once I left Renfrew's residential center, and had selected an eating disorder clinic nearer to my house so that I could live at home and commute to treatment every day. I didn't object to this, though *I* wanted to be the one in charge of making all the phone calls and setting everything up. When my parents rather good-naturedly intervened, I thought they were once more trying to run my life. So I rebelled. I decided that I wanted to continue with day treatment at Renfrew rather than move back home. I insisted that everything would be okay, that I was committed this time around, and they had nothing to worry about.

I was, as it turns out, rather full of shit.

My parents believed me—they had no reason not to. What they didn't realize was, at the time of the argument, I was making the transition from prepared trays to selecting my own food in the cafeteria. Although I had insisted to the doctors I wasn't ready, I was pressured into it, and eventually agreed to fix my own trays without any meal planning in advance. And again, I had shot myself in the foot with my own cleverness. I allowed the staff at Renfrew to think that I was a little more devoted to recovery than I really was. I don't blame them for it—I am, after all, a rather convincing actress—but at the same time, I think they should have listened closer to my protests that I really wasn't ready for this new set of challenges.

The kicker was this—when you stop using trays, staff has no way of monitoring exactly what you eat. There did exist an in-between step, where the counselors weren't looking over your shoulder every five seconds, but your trays were still required to contain the amount of food your meal plan prescribed. When you fixed your own meals, staff took your word on what you had eaten, whether they should have or not.

As my parents argued and I completed my sixth week of treatment, I began to once again approach the one hundred-pound mark, and it scared me. This was significant, not only because of the symbolic meaning of having a triple-digit weight (if I was below one hundred pounds, I could still consider myself an anorexic), but also due to the speed with which I had reached this road marker. My weight had skyrocketed from edema (water retention), due to my extreme state of dehydration from starvation and laxatives. It was miserable. My rings, the ones I fiddled with all day to make sure the circumference of my fingers hadn't magically expanded, became permanently wedged on my hands. As my hormones once again started flowing, I got hot flashes, then night sweats when I would wake up tied in a knot with my sheets, my sopping pajamas clinging to my back. I had started taking birth control pills to jolt my ovaries back into action and consequently had my first period in months. It seemed as if my worst nightmare had come true: weight gain, water retention, menstruation—all at once.

So I dealt with this the only way I knew how—I began to cheat on my menus. Not a lot at first, just a few "substitutions" here and there. I would write down that I had eaten a whole bagel with peanut butter when I really had a slice of toast with jelly. Or a full container of yogurt, when all I had was a carton of 2% milk. And sure enough, within a week, the weight gain slowed, then stalled out completely. My period once again disappeared. As time passed and my meal plan kept getting increased because I wasn't gaining, I realized I would either have to break down and eat, or become more audacious. At first I was worried the other residents might report me, but I gambled on the fact that they were probably so consumed with what was on their trays that they had neither the time nor the inclination to worry about mine. I was right. I started off small—adding lots of hypothetical pats of butter to my rolls, and dumping imaginary creamer into my coffee. Soon, I made more drastic changes. I stopped eating entrees and began to live on chef's salads and cottage cheese. Then, as my confidence grew, I simply started eating as little as I could without being conspicuous. My meal plans got ridiculously large and, simultaneously, so did my lies.

To this day, I don't know if staff ever figured out what was going on. I think they were giving me the benefit of the doubt, though they must have been at least somewhat suspicious. I almost wanted someone to take me aside and ask, "Carrie, what is going on here? How can you be eating *this much* and not gaining an ounce?" I would have confessed—*I was once again a prisoner of my own mind and I wanted out of this cage I had created for myself.* Yet I found myself powerless to say anything. I tried to bring it up with my therapist one day, but the words literally froze on my tongue and I remained silent like I had so many times before.

My anxieties over the whole situation grew to a fever pitch as I stepped down to the day program at Renfrew. I decided against the clinic near my house precisely because I knew it would have been more long-term than staying at Renfrew and that they, more likely than not, would have pigeon-holed me into eating. I knew the Renfrew system well enough to skirt my way around the rules I didn't feel like following. Treatment had, once again, come up short.

I am not disparaging the system at Renfrew, because I think it's one of the best out there. No, it's not perfect, and in the era of managed care, too many women get sent home before their time, making relapse rates, already absurdly high, shoot even higher. I think that there should be more failsafes in these places so that people like me don't slip through the cracks. I did, however, manage to take away a significant number of skills that would serve me later, when I finally committed myself to getting better.

I returned home after completing the day program at Renfrew, and the brief glow of hope I had experienced flickered in the wind and then went black. My old patterns of eating and confronting the world would plague me once again. Wherever you go, there you are. You can't run from yourself. Eventually you tire, and you either quit running or you die. I didn't know this at the time. I didn't know that I would flee from myself one last time before I finally tired of the whole anorexia game and chucked it out the window. I didn't know that all this running was futile and stupid. I just plain didn't know.

And in the space of a few short weeks, I learned.

That was then...

A year has passed since I left Renfrew, and I nearly lost my battle with anorexia. Time seems to have slowed somehow. I don't feel one year older. I feel I have aged ten. I have learned far too much for only one calendar year to have elapsed.

Writing this, I am terrified of the few short steps that stand between me and my eating disorder. It is easy, maybe too easy, to turn back. All that stands between me and utter disaster is my next meal. Yet knowing this does not always mean I am eager to pick up the fork. I watch my chicken noodle soup congeal on the table beside me, determined to forgo slurping this small pleasure. Food haunts me still. Some part of me desperately wishes I could go without eating. Part of me still denies that I, too, need sustenance to survive. I try, in vain, to do without, but each time, I break down and give in, leading to an endless cycle of self-loathing.

Deciding to leave anorexia behind isn't easy. It's a lonely existence, when everyone around you is dieting, and you want to talk about how you're watching your weight, too. But you can't, because you're not. Because you've supposedly risen above that nonsense. You begin to doubt that your body is really okay, begin to toy with anorexic ideas. While friends and family nibble their scoops of cottage cheese and wilted salads with fat-free dressing, you have a hard time ordering a cheeseburger and fries. It is like helping yourself to an all-you-can-eat buffet while you watch a documentary on the starving children in Africa. And you begin to think—it would be so easy. So easy to go back. Just like when you want a box of laxatives. There's the twenty-four hour pharmacy just down the road and you know damned well you can get your desperately needed supplies within. You know what aisle they're in, exactly where they are located on the shelf, which cashiers won't give you strange stares as you purchase five boxes of extra strength chocolate Ex-Lax. You think you will be forever haunted by this knowledge, always held helpless in its thrall.

But one day, you realize that this quest for perfection isn't what it was cracked up to be. You realize that your little game has stripped you of everything you had hoped it would give—your independence, your freedom, your health. So you are left with a choice: wrench yourself free or die. As you have no intention of dying, you begin to pull your way out of anorexia's grasp. And as days turn into weeks, power becomes not the ability to swallow a box of laxatives in one go or eat nothing but pickle relish for three days, but the ability to pass these things by.

Hope is the thing with feathers
That perches in the soul—
And sings the tune without words
And never stops—at all.

Emily Dickinson, "Hope is the Thing with Feathers"

Chapter Eight: Feathers
Winter Into Spring, 2002

On the whole, eating disorder treatment centers are very safe places. Yes, you have to eat, and sometimes you have to eat a lot, two noticeable drawbacks. But you also get to languish in a world where every little thing revolves around food and eating, and, more particularly, around what *you* are eating. You are treated with kid gloves because of your obviously precarious health, and everyone walks on eggshells around you for fear of setting you off. Plus, you don't have to confront the real world—you live in a bubble where the outside world just disappears. For anorexics and bulimics, life doesn't get better than this.

Treatment was an interesting phenomenon. On the one hand, my time at Renfrew gave me the first sense of peace I had in months, even if it didn't last. On the other, it treated the surface symptoms—hideous weight loss, overexercise, and laxative abuse—but left the real problem—a complete deficit of self-esteem—to fester. Sometimes recovery is a crap shoot. My genuine desires to get better, at least at first, blindsided the staff at Renfrew, and they never bothered to confront me when it seemed my energies were waning. I can sit here and spend forever trying to figure out who to blame, but it really doesn't matter. I know help was there for me, had I reached out to it. I only wish it was offered when I needed it.

When I returned home from Renfrew, I had the best of intentions to maintain myself in recovery. I certainly never wanted another trip to a hospital. But I was scared—scared of what the world might bring, scared I couldn't handle it, scared of myself. So backward I slowly slid, until the momentum built and I had no real way to stop myself.

I had originally decided to maintain my discharge weight. As long as my weight didn't go up, everything would be okay. My plans were stymied by the fact that my father had removed the lone scale in our house while I was at Renfrew, so I had no way to weigh myself. In my mind, the only way I could be sure I wasn't *gaining* weight was if I was *losing* it. I didn't intend to lose a lot, not at first, anyway. Just enough to make my pants hang off my butt and to make me, once more, a respectable anorexic.

And so I returned home and found myself holding the pieces of my life, wondering how on earth I was going to put them back together. And once again, I would twirl about in the dance of deception, and use starvation as a means to control my life for one last time.

CR

I started psychotherapy in earnest upon my release, working with a woman who firmly believed in the notion of "tough love." An eating disorder specialist, Susie wasn't above giving me a swift kick in the ass when I needed one, though it was done with care and out of the utmost concern. Sara very much approved of Susie's methods, especially the whole "ass-kicking" technique. Susie gave me back something I didn't even know I had been missing—spunk. I might not have been a wild child, but I was hardly a sheep. An anorexic, though, has no choice but to be a sheep—our disorders tell us exactly what to do, and we are automatons, mindlessly following orders.

I went back to seeing Patrizia, the nutritionist, as well. Returning to her office was surreal. She knew nothing of my restricting at Renfrew (neither did anyone else, for that matter), but she quickly returned me to a meal plan that was more realistic than the one I had been given upon discharge. Had I been ready to really work with her, I'm sure she would have been nothing short of a miracle worker. As it was, we did make some important strides at the time, though some part of me still refused to believe her wise words and gentle advice. I wasn't quite as food-phobic as I had been when we first met, but my fears came in waves. Some days, I almost ate like a "normal" person; other days weren't so reassuring. I didn't know I was entering a period of what is known as "yo-yo dieting," wherein I would lose five pounds, gain it back, freak out, lose it again, gain it back, and so on. This wrecks havoc upon your metabolism, which, due to all the stresses of starvation, essentially shuts down, so I had to eat steadily less and less to maintain my revoltingly low weight.

Not having any other way to entertain myself until I was to return to Hope in January, I decided to get a job at the mall for the holidays. If nothing else, being away from home meant more opportunities to starve myself. I actually rather enjoyed my job. I stuffed teddy bears at the Build-a-Bear Workshop. It was one of those places where people could stuff their own teddy bears, and it was terribly, disgustingly cute. There were lots of little kids around, and I had a grand old time goofing around with them. The best part was when I had to go shopping for the khaki pants I had to wear as a Bear Builder. I smirked the entire time I was in the fitting room. "Mom?" I asked. "The 4 is too big. Can you see if they have a 2? Or grab a 0, maybe?" I loved it. A size 8 or 10 is just, well, so *common* in comparison. I felt special, being so small, and I made sure to speak loudly so everyone nearby would know what size I was wearing.

I packed my own food to take with me when I had to work over mealtimes, using Patrizia's new meal plan as a guide. This is not to say that I actually ate what I packed. I would usually throw half of it away on the way in, and the other half on the way out. My mom had told me to feel free to bring home any food I couldn't eat and she wouldn't yell. What she *would* do, I knew, was worry. I couldn't very well go all day without eating anything and not arouse suspicion and worry. So into the trash my food went. Sometimes, I would stow pieces of fruit and cans of Ensure in my glove compartment, intending to smuggle them back into the house instead of wasting them. This system worked very well until my dad smelled what was up. Literally.

One day, he had to go into my car for something, and, smelling the fruit, he investigated. I can't really blame him for this, because I would have done the exact same thing in his position. I don't think he expected to find what he did. He didn't say anything at first, he just left the fruit and cans of Ensure on the kitchen table. *Oh, shit...* I thought about it for a minute. There really was no good explanation for this. I knew the "I'm just saving it for a rainy day" excuse would not fly.

"What," my father asked me, "were you going to do with the fruit?"

"Ummmm… bring it back inside?" I suggested weakly. I tried to smile.

"So why did you leave it in your car?"

"I was waiting for the right time."

"The right time being when your mother and I wouldn't be watching."

"Well, if you really want to know… yes… it was something along those lines."

He *harrumph*ed. He stared at the ground for a minute, examining the linoleum on the kitchen floor. "Why can't you eat any of this?" he asked quietly. He looked up at me, his blue eyes searching mine.

It was my turn to stare at the floor. "I don't want to gain weight," I said softly. "I'm so fat as it is, I just thought that… well… I *couldn't* eat all this."

By this time, my mom had joined the fray. She said, "Sweetie, you're barely breaking one hundred pounds as it is. You're hardly fat. And you're supposed to be gaining weight." How could I explain that *she* wasn't the one who had to look at herself in the mirror at the end of the day and make peace with everything she had eaten?

I don't really remember how the argument ended. I know my parents told me to stop wasting food, and to talk about my fears with Susie and Patrizia. I promised I would, though I had no real intention of doing so. After this, I changed tactics slightly. Instead of stashing food in my glove compartment, I would throw half of my lunch away and bring the other half home. I don't think my parents believed me when I said I had eaten the rest, but what could they really do?

Sara called once, while I was at work, and my mom let slip that I was hiding food *and* that Susie had suggested another hospitalization to stem the trickle of a weight loss that was turning into a torrent. I did not know about their conversation, and, when we met at the bookstore near our houses in December, I was greeted by a slap across the face. I was too startled to do anything. Sara then gave me a big bear hug. "What are you *doing* to yourself? You have to stop this. You can't keep going from hospital to hospital to hospital." I wanted to say, what *else* am I going to do? But she kept going. "If you don't make it back to Hope, *who is going to be my roommate?* Who is going to keep my head screwed on straight? Who is going to run around Holland with me and steal tulips at Tulip Time? Who is going to help me yank the heads off Barbie dolls?" I didn't know what to say.

To be honest, I was planning to go back to Hope in January for the same reason I went earlier that fall: to lose weight. I didn't really want to go back to the hellish grind of classes and studying. My friends and I, already separated by the gap of my study abroad in Scotland, were now divided by the gaping chasm of my eating disorder and subsequent semester away in treatment. I felt that I didn't have anything in common with them anymore. It makes me sad to think about it, and to think of all the interesting people I could have met during those wasted semesters, but didn't. In moments when I struggle to stay in recovery, I try to think of things like this, of what anorexia has taken away from me, and what she will continue to take unless I put a stop to her. As hokey as it sounds, there are simply too many books to be read and songs to be sung to be caught in the all-consuming passion of the size of your butt.

Nevertheless, at that time, my weight continued to drop. And drop. Susie eventually put her foot down and flipped when, on Christmas Eve, I waltzed in having lost seven pounds in the previous week. I didn't drink bucketfuls of water that day because I honestly didn't think I had lost any weight, or, if I had, it was only a pound or two. With my weight once again hovering around ninety pounds, she gave me the phone number of the intake specialist at Beaumont Hospital, and I found myself looking down my nose at yet another inpatient hospital stay.

That day, I went to work at Build-a-Bear, throwing away all of my lunch because my mom had planned a special Christmas Eve dinner, and I was, once again, back on my five hundred calorie per day diet. I spent the day trying to figure out how to break the news to my mother. I couldn't very well walk in the door and say, "Merry Christmas, Mom! Guess where I get to go?" She knew I was headed in that direction, but she didn't think I would get there so fast.

My parents were devastated by the news, and even my brother asked me, "What are we going to have to do to get you better?" Christmas that year was depressing. Everyone tried to celebrate in good cheer, but it was a false, hollow kind of cheer, and it only served to make the day more depressing. Events happened much quicker after the 25th. And, because my psychiatrist had agreed to the need for inpatient care, I didn't need an evaluation in advance. So, on December 27, I was admitted to Beaumont Hospital.

My parents followed me up to the ninth floor of the hospital, the locked psych unit, with a dazed and horrified look. I've seen this look at every place I've been to. It always reads—how could this happen to us, to our child? Has it really come to this? Why didn't we do a better job, why didn't we stop this? What is going to happen now? Up until this point, life had seemed almost bucolic. Now, not only is our child sick, but she's likely Looney Tunes as well.

This can be rather hard to swallow in one gulp. It can take a long time to sink in, and some parents never quite grasp it.

New admits to an eating disorder program always breed a peculiar kind of terror for the other eating disordered patients, the kind of nightmare that finds you sitting bolt upright, sweating and gasping for air. And it's not because we're anti-social and don't like meeting people. We're just afraid of what the competition might bring, that we might not be the thinnest person, or the one who has lost the most weight, or the one with the worst story. It's profoundly unsettling, to have your whole self-concept turned on its head by one person walking down the hallway, and so the news of pending arrivals typically evokes trepidation at best and hostility at worst.

The nurse who admitted me gave me a tour of the unit, pointing out the communal showers (Oh, dear God—not again) and the water cooler. I mumbled a quiet hello to the other patients, not knowing what else to say. I walked by two unmarked doors, one on either side of the hallway, and peered in. There was no furniture inside. Nothing. Just four walls, a ceiling, and a floor. Then it all sank in with a resounding *clunk*. These were rooms with padded walls. I thought that practice only existed in old movies, the ones with straight jackets and shots from Nurse Ratchet. What the hell kind of place *was* this? Starving yourself to death was crazy, but not *this* crazy.

I met my roommate, a face I recognized from attending the Beaumont support group. Cathy didn't look that sick at first glance, though I soon found out that looks could be *very* deceiving. She was already hooked up to an I.V. and I vaguely wondered whether one would be ordered for me. On the one hand, the I.V. was (as I learned from Cathy) almost pure fat, which sounded downright revolting, never mind that it would make me gain weight faster. I sure as hell didn't want that. On the other hand, an I.V. would officially mean that I was too thin, pleasing my anorexic little heart. That I was, once again, signing myself into a mental institution because I could not bring myself to eat failed to register with me.

I still have mixed feelings about hyperalimentation.[14] I am recovered enough to realize that I was lucky my situation hadn't gotten so dire as to require an I.V., that it meant less suffering on my behalf and

---

[14] Hyperalimentation is the "official" medical word for intravenously administered nutrition and sustenance.

that of my family and friends. Time has, as it usually does, given me a much broader perspective on things. That being said, I feel almost gypped out of an I.V. It was a status symbol in the messed-up world of eating disorders, sort of like owning a Jaguar or Porsche. How many feeding tubes have *you* had, we asked each other, constantly feeling out the competition so we knew who we had to beat next time. The person with the most forced feedings won. It's a stupid and petty little game, to be sure, but when you're stuck in a hospital with a bunch of similarly crazy sick people, there is nonetheless some sort of draw to it.

Living in a mental ward does strange things to your head, sometimes stranger than the things that got you there in the first place. You begin to believe that hours spent doodling in coloring books or chatting in group therapy is perfectly normal. You begin to think that everyone talks with patronizing "I Feel" statements. You forget that a real world exists outside the doors of the unit, that everyone else is getting on with their lives while you languish in your own melodrama. You wonder how you're going to survive in the "real world" once you're discharged, the same way you once wondered how you were going to survive the psych ward. But the reason is simple—we adapt. The unthinkable becomes the mundane. Adaptation is how we survive these hellish conditions with a scrap of our minds intact.

The ninth floor of Beaumont was a bizarre little reflection of the mentally normal, only everything was more sharp, painted more vividly, the lines exaggerated. Most psych patients tend to be very intense and very choleric, and it is the combination of these two qualities that usually require us to be locked up. It was almost like a family atmosphere—cranky older people, and lots of good-natured teasing from the younger ones. What I found comforting was that I could always count on someone to be more messed-up than I was. Sometimes, I almost felt normal, well-adjusted, which I found particularly hilarious.

The familial ambience was especially noticeable at mealtime, when we all sat down and ate together. Like the other places I'd been treated in, our days revolved around eating, though for different reasons if you were in the eating disorder program. If your relationship with food was not at all morbid, you would mark your day by breakfast, lunch, and dinner, because these were the most notable features of the day. They were the only things that changed from day to day, the only way you had to mark the inexorable passage of time. For the rest of us, it was another matter entirely.

When I first arrived at Beaumont, I was not informed of my treatment plan, and thus I wasn't in the position of officially being "forced" to eat. I picked at my breakfast and lunch, one eye on Cathy and her plate, not wanting to eat more than her, but at the same time trying to remember that she had an I.V. I noticed how she closely followed what I had eaten, staying precisely one step behind me so she could still say to herself that she had eaten less. I was curious how long I could keep this up. The doctor in charge had a philosophy of "food as medicine," so I kind of doubted it would be another repeat of Rogers. As it turned out, I was right.

One of the nurses pulled me aside after the last group session at the end of my first day. "Carrie," he said, "because you haven't been eating all your food, you've been put on tray sitting."

What in the bloody *hell* was that? I asked him this, wondering what wretched fate lay in store for me. Could it be any worse than eating all of that nasty hospital food? I shuddered. I soon found out that tray sitting was a wonderful behavior modification tool invented by the lovely psychiatrist in charge of the eating disorder patients. If you didn't eat all of your meal *and* you refused your supplement of Ensure Plus, then you had to sit in front of your tray until you either finished your food or your next tray arrived. I didn't have a problem with this little arrangement until I learned two things: 1) staff would confiscate any book I brought to the table and 2) any visitors I had were turned away at the door of the unit. Including my parents.

I remember calling home, hysterical and sobbing, telling my mother not to bother coming that night, as they were trying to force me to eat the food. There was a slight pause on her end of the line—Well, yes, dear, that's what they're *supposed* to be doing. She said she understood why I was so incensed, but still encouraged me to eat my dinner. "You don't have to eat all of the shit they bring you!" I yowled into the phone. Later, Cathy pointed out to me that the sooner I ate the food they brought me in here, the sooner I could get out and go back to not eating. Well, then. I mulled this over for a while, realized she had a point. I sighed and capitulated for the time being, silently outraged at my evil doctor's plotting.

Don't get me wrong—I genuinely liked this doctor, and still admire and respect him to this day, especially for being the first "expert" to treat me with simple human compassion. He is, after all, still my doctor. But the whole tray sitting incident left me rather irate for a number of days. I realize now, too, the deeper motivations Cathy may have had in persuading me to eat. If I ate, then it was okay for her to eat, too. And I think, deep down, she really did want to eat, but she somehow needed permission, whether from the doctor or from me, before she would allow herself to pick up her fork.

And then I saw the tray they had sent up for me.

I glanced at the menu, did a double take. Fish nuggets. Deep-fried fish? And, God help me, French fries! *What did these flaming idiots put on my plate?* I vowed to hunt down the nutritionist at the hospital and give her a sound thrashing. Didn't they know better than to give me, the anorexic extraordinaire of the ninth floor, all of this nasty, lipid-laden food? It was bad enough I had to eat, but I wouldn't have even touched this junk *before* my eating disorder, let alone since my eating habits had become diagnostically pathological. I angrily stabbed each one of my nuggets, by then soggy and cold, before moving on to the fries—also soggy and cold—and lastly the peas, which I proceeded to mush up in the middle of my plate before I nibbled at my quasi-pea pond from the outside in.

My parents did come to visit that night, bringing with them an emergency e-mail letter (a kick in the ass, as she would describe it later) from Sara. Sara had called my house to chat with me not long after I had spoken with my mom earlier that day. She was dutifully informed that I had landed my sorry self back in the hospital. She knew I was on a crash course in that direction, of course, but she didn't realize things had actually gotten that bad. So Sara forwarded the letter to my mother to bring to me. I sat down on my bed after visiting hours were over, and started reading.

"To be or not to be, that is the question: whether 'tis nobler in the mind to starve oneself to death or to actually give a rat's ass..."

The email continued, *"You say you are trying—that's a lie! You say you never do anything half-assed, then why is it you are TRYING HALF-ASSED?! Hell, I don't even think that you are trying at all! I know you, you are a lot more than you give yourself credit for. I think you are scared. What if I try and don't succeed, will I be a failure then?' Is it safer to be the perfect little anorexic girl? What will we say at your funeral? 'I've never met a better anorexic than her—she pretended to try to get better, but she never actually did try.' That is the most un-noble death I have ever seen. The little children who die in the hospital from AIDS, cancer, or leukemia are far better than the death you have chosen. All they want is to be healthy—that is a far cry from what you say to yourself.*

"Do you even think about the future anymore? You used to talk about it all the time. I miss your little fantasies about getting your Ph.D., working on Ebola, and having kids with Celtic names who can't ice skate and hate Barbies. You never think about that anymore. All you think about is if you land your ass in the hospital maybe you will be good enough then. Your worst fear—being a failure,

being a coward. Well that is exactly what you are doing now. The girl who was too
scared to TRY, the girl who couldn't even succeed at the most basic of things—
keeping herself alive. And don't try to tell me you are not on the path to death—
you know that is exactly where you are going!

 "Do you know I actually give a shit about you? You may not understand it
or see what I see, but if you make the right choice, you will someday—that is a
PROMISE. Do you know I actually prayed for you? Do you know how long it
has been since I actually prayed for someone? You may not believe in God now. But
do this for me: acknowledge that if, by some random chance, there is a God, you will
let Her help you. You may not believe, you may have closed Her off—but just
humor me. You don't have to pray, just don't block Her out like you have everything else.

 "Even if you think I am full of shit, you are full of way more of it than
I…[and] I will not let you continue on that Amtrak without first trying my
damndest to flag it down."

I sat on my hard hospital bed while I read this, over and over and
over again, absorbing the words into my skin in sort of a primeval
literary osmosis. I was struck, first, by the anger in the note. But the
more I read Sara's words, the more I began to understand the deep love
behind what she had to say. Even though I had stopped believing I
could be anything without anorexia, she, like my parents, had not, and
was not about to let me take the easy way out. Distractedly, I watched
the headlights of the busy Detroit traffic as they sped by me many
stories below.

As I sat on my bed, I thought about my life, about what had
become of me. I thought of my friends, eagerly awaiting the start of
their final semester at Hope, the simple joys in their lives. I thought of
the people driving in the cars below me, how they didn't give a rip
about nasty fish nuggets and mean doctors and stubborn anorexics. I
thought of my vocabulary, how limited it had become, how everything
I thought was framed in the context of "hungry," or "thin," or "food."
I thought of how pathetic my life had become, of all the things
anorexia had stolen from me and all the things she would continue to
take. I realized I missed my friends and my former life, and, God help
me, I wanted to take them back. It finally dawned on me that anorexia
was not my friend, she was my enemy—she had stripped me of the
very things I was trying to attain. Mostly, though, I thought about how
I was simply sick and tired of living like this.

At that moment, I channeled all of the negative emotions swirling
around me, and decided to give anorexia the boot. The anger from all
of this burned a hole in my middle, the bright orange glow of stoked

coals, and I knew anorexia's days were numbered. For the first time, I realized I wanted more than this farce of a life I had created for myself. When push came to shove, I decided that I would rather live, however fraught with peril life may be, than die a miserable death all by myself in some random hospital. To succeed at anorexia is to fail at life, and, as Sara wrote, I am *not* a failure.

CR

Don't tell me it's too late
'cause I've relied on my illusion
To keep me warm at night
And I've denied in my capacity to love
But I am willing to give up this fight.

Sarah McLachlan, "Dirty Little Secret"

From there on out, things changed. For the first time, I genuinely wanted to get better, from the inside out, and I actively worked at recovery. I didn't particularly want to gain weight, but I went along with it because I couldn't stand all of anorexia's side effects. I ate the food with relatively little protest. I gained weight, pound by pound, simultaneously gaining life. Even my steps lightened. I went to groups. Some days, I actually participated. I stopped hiding behind a book, though I still managed to do an inordinate amount of reading. And I began to feel something that I thought had left me entirely, the flicker of a candle in a bitterly cold winter's night—hope. I was bound and determined to get better.

This is not to say, of course, that I didn't have my down moments. I did. Especially when the side effects of re-feeding hit me head-on once again. I experienced intense physical pain when eating because, once again, my stomach had shrunk to a piteously small size. Only this time, I had medication to encourage my stomach to empty, so that I could actually eat what was on my trays. My digestive system was so sluggish that the food I ate basically just sat there, undigested, in my intestines. My body literally had no idea what to do with food in my system, and it took a lot of time and medication before I could eat a meal and have it move through my digestive tract in a normal amount of time. I envisioned my intestines, snake-like, wrapping themselves around the ridiculous amount of food I had to eat, eagerly wringing every last calorie out of my meals. Pooping was cause for celebration on the unit. "Guess what, everybody! I took a dump!" we would shriek, as we danced circles around the ninth floor. My fingers swelled, and I began to sweat. A lot. Like, disgustingly a lot, as my metabolism and the production of hormones surged upward once again.

I soon tired of all this. When people heard I had to gain weight, they thought that it sounded kind of fun. And, to be honest with you, I originally thought that it would be a breeze, too. All I had to do was eat a couple extra pieces of pie and the weight would just magically appear. Wrong. By the time I was discharged from Beaumont, I was eating upwards of four thousand calories per day to induce even a modest weight gain. Imagine all the food you eat in the course of a day. Now double it. That was my daily reality. Do this all day, every day, for weeks, months. Not so fun, is it? Stuffing yourself or eating with pure abandon is fun every now and then, but it gets very old, very fast, even when your very life depends upon it.

But gain weight I slowly did and, after my weight inched its way up, my pulse strengthened, and my blood pressure hauled itself back onto the charts, my insurance company kicked me out of the hospital and sent me instead to the day program. The morning of my departure, as I was packing my belongings in my suitcase, I decided, for no particular reason, to bring my stuffed moose (representing the spirit of Moose the dog) from Build-a-Bear with me to morning group. My moose, Casey, who was named after my Atlanta roommate, had a little sound box in its paw that you could press to elicit hysterical giggles, though staff had failed to notice when they searched my stuff on the first day. I was demonstrating this to a woman on bedrest, who looked like she could use a laugh, when one of the nurses, Ron, stopped me and my giggling moose in the hallway. He acted like a prissy little girl, hands on hips, threatening to tell Mommy if I didn't stop it right this second. He was nice enough, to be sure, but he was also a stickler for the rules. This irritated the hell out of me, so I relished moments where I could annoy him in return. "Just what," he asked haughtily, "do you have there?"

"Um, a stuffed moose?" Was this not obvious?

"What is in that moose?"

"Um, fluff?"

"What is in that moose that is making that noise?" Ron got more exasperated by the second and I swore I saw his hands twitch towards his hips.

"Oh, that. That's just a giggle sound in the paw that you can press. See?" I sent Casey into another fit of laughter as I held her up for him to inspect.

"How does the sound work?" His dry, clinical tone began to get on my nerves, and I had to restrain myself from giving the son-of-a-bitch a good slap. Instead, I shrugged my shoulders. Was I supposed to know?

"If it's battery-operated, I'm going to have to take it. Unit rules."

I hunched protectively over Casey. "What am I going to do—electrocute myself in the shower with my own damned moose? Good God—I don't even have scissors to cut the threads to yank the sound box out!" He merely sighed. I wished I'd had one of those bullhorns, the kind policemen used when they make a big arrest in the movies, so I could yell, "STEP AWAY FROM THE MOOSE! STEP AWAY FROM THE MOOSE AND NO ONE GETS HURT!" They had already taken my freedom, which I couldn't precisely blame them for, but they were not going to lay a finger on my moose. Had they actually tried to take Casey away from me, I think I would have thrown a fit and had to have been locked up in one of those padded rooms.

Luckily, the nurse had a shred of common sense and let Casey be, primarily because I was going home that afternoon and I would have opportunities aplenty to shock myself with the sound box in my own shower. I mean, I understand staff has to keep us safe and all, but this seemed a little ridiculous. So Casey and I were discharged from the ninth floor with (relatively) little fuss, and I moved back into my room at our house on Willow Road.

The day after I was discharged I began an independent study for my senior project on feminism and the cultural construction of the body, wasting no time getting back into the swing of things. The registrar at Hope, bless his little heart, knew of my situation and the reasons for my sudden withdrawal from the spring semester as well, and matched me with an English professor who specialized in this topic. It was a match made in heaven, and who knows—it just may have been.

But, before I began my last semester of classwork in earnest, it was back to treatment for me. The three weeks I spent in the day program were relatively unremarkable. It was intended more as a maintenance program than specific therapy. I didn't have any earth-shattering revelations while I was there, nor did my attitude towards recovery turn a 180, or, in my case, a 360. What I can say is this—it was invaluable in helping me stabilize at my discharge weight. I had gained ten pounds during my week at Beaumont, a mere drop in the bucket when you're forty to fifty pounds underweight, but the weight gain was achieved rather rapidly, and I had a very different type of body to get used to. Unbeknownst to staff, I snuck a glance at my chart, and so I knew exactly how much I weighed, though this actually made me feel better—I thought I had gained much more weight than I really had. But I got the best of both worlds at this weight, because I was definitely still slim, even slimmer than society would call "attractive," but I also knew I was out of immediate medical danger.

I try to go back and think of what made this time different, why treatment finally worked when it had failed so many times before. I had finally grown bored with the tiring melodrama of anorexia and decided I should write my own script. My existence was no longer a cheap puppet show on a sideshow stage. I refused to play the anorexic for a couple of quarters from the audience. No, I was director, producer, and star all rolled into one and, dammit, that's the way it was supposed to be. Recovery, in some sense, is about sitting up and taking control of your life. It's about not letting Mommy, Daddy, and the world tell you what to do and how to act and what you want. I am learning how to disagree with people, learning that people don't automatically hate my guts when I think differently than they do. I was airing out my emotional bedding, shining a light onto the piles of dirty laundry in my psyche where the shaggy, hairy monsters lived.

Eating disorders don't breed in the spotlight, they flourish in the dim corners of our secret lives. Our behaviors, so cloaked in shame and fear and hopelessness, fester unseen because we are too scared to let anyone else know what's going on. Letting those skeletons out of the closet takes a particular kind of courage, the kind of steadfast bravery of storybook heroes. We have every excuse in the book (and then some) not to keep going, to up and quit, to throw in the towel. But we don't, because we believe in our fight and, ultimately, ourselves. That is how the battle is won, not with the mass conversions of people at anti-eating-disorder speeches and feminist rallies, but with a sort of grassroots movement of one woman, followed by another, and then another, saying, "I am more than what I weigh."

Eating disorder prevention, though a noble goal, has a long way to go. Scare tactics don't work, not really. Because no one ever thinks that they will be the one to get trapped in a funhouse mirror filled hell. More than that, at the outset, dying is fun. Dying is exciting. Especially to intense people questioning the meaning of life. Dying is something that, if you do it right, you only get to do once. So what *should* we do to prevent these deadly disorders? We debunk the bullshit spewed at us by the billion-dollar diet industry. We tell our stories in the vain hope that one of you will learn from one of us, that maybe our lives won't have completely gone to waste. We owe it to those teetering on the edge to paint our disorders in their true colors, not glossing over the gruesome parts and turning our stories into some grand retelling of *Rebecca of Sunnybrook Farm*. Instead, our stories are more of a *Pulp Fiction*-meets-*Schindler's List*-blockbuster: a realistic, in-your-face, gripping account of a life gone to ruin, a heart-wrenching tale of anger and despair and, somehow, salvation amidst the wreckage.

In the end, the only thing that will save you is your willingness to take life head-on. I never said you had to be good at it, just willing to try, willing to give life a chance. Eventually, if you don't get good at confronting life's difficulties, you will get good at faking it, and, as they say, fake it 'till ya make it. Eating disorders cannot stand up to the carefree attitude of a budding life, the freedom of "Why the hell not!" It's the road not taken for me, and it has made all the difference, all the difference in the world.

Remember this—it's your life. And you only get one shot at it.

You save yourself or you remain unsaved.

Alice Sebold, *Lucky*

Chapter Nine: Salvation
Winter Into Spring 2002

I t was nothing short of a miracle. On the surface, we looked like three typical college-aged women eating breakfast together. We turned the stove on a little too high, burning the apple cinnamon pancakes, and accidentally left the muffins doughy and soft in the center. Beneath the exterior, we were three women with eating disorders making a desperate attempt to pretend that we were not still ravaged by the remnants of our disease. We pretended to add a few teaspoons of cooking oil to the muffin batter, and kindly overlooked everyone's refusal to ask for a pat of butter for the pancakes. But, together, we shared a meal.

We sat and chatted as we sipped our black coffee, discussing what we were planning to do with our lives once college was over. As we spoke of our struggles, I wondered what other demons haunted my classmates, how many other people would carry an eating disorder with them as they accepted their degrees. My other achievements, my awards—my GPA—pale in comparison to what I have lived through with my eating disorder.

For three women terrified to admit their hunger, this momentous act of eating had become nothing short of mind-bending. For those millions more like us, the simple task of nourishing their own bodies still remains a complex snarl of right and wrong, should I or shouldn't I?

Though I am no longer ill enough to deny myself food on a regular basis, I am not yet well enough to give my body all the nutrients it needs. I live in limbo-land, a kind of Purgatory for the anorexic. But each day it gets harder to remember my nightmare, each day the behaviors slip further and further from my grasp. And each day, I move further and further into the Great Beyond, that land of recovery that waits for us all.

ᏨᎡ

Recovery is a complex concept to embrace. It's simple and yet it isn't, but it always stems from the realization that anorexia is a sinking ship. Starving myself was never the means to keep my boat from going under. My sticking point was believing that constantly bailing out bucketfuls of water from my little rowboat was somehow stronger and better than radioing for help. This was my warped way of thinking, and anorexia twisted my psyche until I thought that losing was winning and hunger was pride. The people who recover from an eating disorder, and I *do* believe in the possibility of complete recovery, have all had the courage to speak up and say, "Something's not working here. I want out."

So we strap on our life preservers and jump ship, knowing that we will be swimming toward an unknown shore. We tread water by the boat for a dreadfully long time, waiting, hoping that the hapless boat will miraculously right itself and we can clamor back in. It never does, but that never stops us from hoping. Realizing that my boat was a lost cause kicked me in the stomach and knocked the air out of me, leaving me stunned, breathless. *What am I going to do now?* If I wanted to live, I had one choice—follow those voices calling to me in the distance, or let the eating disorder pull me under and finally come to rest in a watery grave.

Thus we swim, knowing neither our final destination nor who we will meet when we reach the shore. The courageous solution has been there all the time, staring us in the face. *Get out of the boat, dammit! Get out of the boat and swim for shore!* And here we were, thinking that sinking with the ship was the true sign of strength. In reality, sinking is the coward's way out. Going down with your ship is the easy solution to the leaky boat problem.

Have I reached the shore? I don't know. I do know that my

current location in this river is much more shallow and calm than the river of anorexia.

But the road to recovery is not a neatly paved interstate highway. On your good days, the road is dirt. On the bad ones, it's an ocean of mud that grasps onto your four-wheel drive tires and won't let go. You take wrong turns. Your car breaks down. Sometimes, your CB radio breaks and you are left stranded in the middle of the Amazon rain forest. Helga, the hijacker of my brain, didn't just pack up and leave because I suddenly found her annoying. She did strange things to try to get me back in her grasp, showed me all the tricks, pulled out all the stops. I did things I thought I would never do: barfing, cutting, going back to restricting. All in the name of recovery. Yet in order to move forward, we must accept the risk of going the wrong way, and have to humble ourselves to find the way back to our original path.

January 2002

I was trying to find pants in the mall.

I passed The Limited Too, and felt a strange pang. I remember exulting at being able to shop in a girls' store. Never mind that the pants were both too short and too juvenile for me to wear. No, that didn't matter to me. Before, I would waltz by store windows, knowing that the only clothes with a chance of fitting me resided in the children's section. Size 0 had become too large, because the fashion designers assume, even at that size, that women have something resembling a butt.

Which, by the way, I didn't.

Now I walked by the very same store and stopped dead in my tracks. My heart lurched and sank to the pit of my stomach. I was too massive for girls' clothing. Oh, help me, Jesus, what have I done? Part of me wailed in grief, a primal scream of unbearable agony. I searched frantically for myself, my identity, *anything* at all to reassure my mind that I was still there. The whole of me had been diluted—the same person now occupies more space. The chocolate smoothie relished only minutes before now resided in my stomach like a rock. Guilt rushed in, pressed against the dam, flowed over. Detached, I watched the gangly twelve-year-old girls browse with their mothers. I bickered with the Nazi bitch in my skull. A grown woman should not be shopping in the kids' department. Yeah, but I'm special...

A lifetime of memories flashed before my eyes, leaving my hollowed insides gasping for air. Then, with a tangible sorrow, I gathered my coat in my arms, turned my back to the store, and slowly walked away, each step carrying me farther and farther from my eating disorder.

CR

The media has the rather bad habit of glamorizing eating disorders, of making them sound like something "everyone" does. We devour gossip over which celebrities are starving themselves, their maniacal exercise routines, and other ways they maintain their size 2 figures (it's called airbrushing, by the way). Hey, if it's safe for movie stars, then it's safe for me, right? All we see are the cute, skinny little bodies and the voice that chirps, "Oh, I'm still a healthy eater, but I'm all over eating disorder stuff now. That was *so* last year." We somehow never hear of the bowls of Corn Flakes that provoked anxiety attacks, of the weak, rubbery knees that threatened to give out from under them as they dragged their exhausted (but skinny) asses off the Stairmaster. No one ever seems to mention that, the vast expanse that lies between "sick" and "better," and how damn likely it is to lose your way in this wasteland.

Part of the problem with this glamorization, too, lies in the sheer number of people who have experimented with eating disorders. It has almost become a rite of passage: go to high school, get anorexia, go off to college, get married, have children, *et al*. All in a life's work. The examples all around us have, in a sense, become so much a part of our cultural scenery that it's no longer possible to point your finger at the perpetrators. Because we're all guilty, in a sense. We have all, at some point in our lives, bought into the cultural dogma that skinny is happy and fat is evil. I almost wish this were true; if it were, I would have been one of the most goddamned happy people I know. The fact remains that these are lies, hollow half-truths that threaten to steal our lives, our very existence, right out from under us. It's as if we've all fallen victim to some sort of a mass delusion that losing is winning and giving up means selling out.

And you wonder why I'm jaded.

I hate that I once believed this bullshit. I'm embarrassed that I fell for the trickery, the deception that a can of some gritty, chalky shake was lunch. I shudder every time I crack open a can of Diet Coke and encourage the Industry, because I can't yet bring myself to drink regular soda. I pray to a God that I'm no longer sure I believe in that I haven't inadvertently encouraged someone to follow in my footsteps. Writing this book is one of the ways I hope to make sure this never happens. Oh, I know damn well that some of you reading these words, right here, right now, are still thinking about giving anorexia or bulimia a whirl. Just to see if it works. To tell you the truth, it does—if you're trying to create a life of misery. And that's all you're ever going to get. Going around bursting bubbles breaks my heart, but I can hardly sit around and leave people to the same fate I once upon a time fashioned for myself.

I've been told, many times, that I need to view myself and my abilities in a more realistic fashion. I am human. I am not flawless. I do not have to be. This new mantra of mine hums constantly in my brain. I have recorded over the old messages that hissed, "Do it better! Be perfect!" Disabusing myself of these notions takes work, more work than I ever believed could be funneled into one single endeavor. Not that my recovery has been totally *sans* the occasional epiphany, but it has come more from the gradual, slow march of time than from any divine revelation.

Many view recovery as the moment in which one could take no more of his or her disorder, and decided to up and quit. This is more distorted thinking. Though there is probably some truth to it, it is more accurate to cite this as a moment of strength, the beginning of a mental shift, when we stopped playing victim to our disease. Most of us fell into our disorders with a minimal amount of help. I knew what I was doing, and I figured it out on my own. It took months of therapy, countless false starts, and the combined knowledge of dozens of experts for me to see the light of recovery. Falling into the trap of anorexia was the easy part, freeing myself, a much more laborious process.

February 2002

...and then I sit back, and it hits me—all of the food I've eaten, the empty boxes and wrappers, the crumbs strewn everywhere.

I lean down and stare into the empty toilet bowl as if it were my soul. So empty. So pristine. I feel so dirty, full of impurities. I take a deep, ragged breath, steady my nerves and slow my pulse, and carefully lift the seat. It is a self-fulfilled prophecy, you see, the sweet oblivion I find as I rid myself of everything foul and base. If only I hadn't been such a pig and eaten the *entire box of cereal*, the whole goddamn box, bowl after bowl until I was madly shoveling crumbs into my mouth. I sit back and stare at the empty box of Cookie Crisp and the empty milk carton, the horror of what I have done beginning to dawn on me. But I don't stop. No, in my twisted mind, the only way out of this mess is to keep eating. I move on to the half-full carton of ice cream, the cookies and Pop-Tarts. Anything, really, that I can hastily shove into my mouth, searching, like a demon possessed, for something else to fill the gaping emptiness inside.

Eventually, I run out of steam, if not food. Taking the wrappers and boxes, I shove them deep down into the garbage can, hoping that if I push them far enough my binge will disappear. I survey my waste-land of cupboards. How empty it all looks—I will have to go shopping tomorrow to stock up for the next binge. But until then... Until then I will have to deal with the reality of what I have done. And so I find myself in the bathroom, staring into the toilet bowl. For a brief second, I lay my flushed cheek on the cool porcelain and blink, knowing what has to be done.

So I take my position in firm command of the toilet, lower my head down and slide my first two fingers down my throat. Nothing happens. Shit. I poke a little harder, then even faster and more insistently until I find the gag spot. Holding my hand in place, my mistakes come rushing back up at me, and relief, along with an almost holy ecstasy, floods through me. This cycle of vomiting and rejoicing continues, and I idly realize that my fingers must be halfway down my throat by now. I wish, more than anything, that I could shove my hand all the way down and pull the food back out myself. Instead I will have to content myself with my own personal vomitorium. As my toilet fills with half-digested junk food, the growing emptiness in my gut soothes my jagged nerves. Relief, at last—I have finally fixed my mistake. In order to be sure I have rid myself of every last scrap of food, I chug glass after glass of water, that elixir of life that is now helping to kill me. Then I barf again, washing my insides out.

I am still sitting in front of the porcelain goddess, only now I am empty and it is full. I idly watch chunks of Pop-Tart float around in the bowl, bobbing up and down, as I stare, aghast, at the amount of food I have just eaten. Regardless of how appetizing the contents of my stomach were on the way down, they look considerably less so after they have come back up. The acrid, stale reek of vomit clings in the air, making me want to barf all over again. Spraying the can of Glade with one hand, I flush with the other, again and again and again, until no trace of food is left. Then I grab the scrub brush and scour out the toilet. It's a ritual, you see, and it brings comfort to my maddening distress, as much as it is torment in and of itself. I wish I could flush away the memories of what I have just done, but they don't swirl away so easily. Wandering my apartment, I realize that my only escape is the same trap of bulimia in which I am ensnared. I am damned by my salvation. So I sit back and wonder once more how long I will last until my dirty little secret bubbles to the surface, and I lose control and binge once more.

ᏉᏒ

Other women have asked me how I managed to keep picking myself up after each and every fall during recovery. I tell them that the dull ache that trails your every move can be endured. The skies cannot storm forever, and sunlight will come again.

Yes, you fear. But you grit your teeth. Take a breath. Steady. Forward. Faith. Keep moving. Silently, swiftly. You edge one foot forward. You open your eyes. Inhale. Faith. You stumble onward, gasp for air. Before you are even aware of the events surrounding you, the journey is over. And you are free.

Then you jump, taking a flying leap off a momentous cliff, and dive into the unknown. You fall, knowing you may hit the ground. You fall, trusting other people to break your rapid descent. Air rushes past your face as terror tightens its hold on your insides. The fall is long, so dreadfully long that you begin to wonder if you will survive the landing. And for one breathless moment, you fear no one will be there to catch you.

But there always is.

I was lucky. My parents always stayed close to break my fall, as did Sara and my treatment team. I can't thank them enough for that. But the important thing is not having someone around to catch you. It's learning to stand on your own two feet.

March 2002

I face my sandwich. It's just you and me, buster. Two pieces of bread, two ounces of turkey (99 percent fat free), stacked on top of each other. Me and my lunch.

I am patently aware that I can't bring myself to eat it. My throat literally closes up, and an invisible hand tightens around my stomach. I scrutinize the Zip-Loc baggy from all angles, trying to determine if a dab of mayonnaise could have made its way onto the bread and from thence to my stomach.

Distract yourself from the food. It's not that big of a deal. It's only *lunch*, only a bloody sandwich. But it's a lunch I don't have to eat. Not if I don't want to. I am *in control* of the situation here. I choose whether or not Wonder Bread and Butterball will pass between my lips. Houston, we don't have a problem.

Leave the sandwich on the table. See? You're strong. Yes, you're *strong*. I rummage through my purse, select a book. I pretend to read Jane Austen. Words swim on the page: turkey, turkey, bread, yum. I give the sandwich a dirty look. Shut *up*, I'm *trying* to read here. I snatch the baggy and shove it back into the brown paper bag. Out of sight, out of mind.

Yeah, right. To eat or not to eat, that is the question.

I look from the garbage can to my lunch and back again. I realize the sandwich would be far better off in the trash bin than in my stomach. Kids are starving in Africa, you *bitch*. You pack yourself a happy little lunch that you never had any intention of eating, and now you're *wasting* all of this *food*.

I glance furtively around the room. Anyone watching? No? I snatch the sandwich out of the bag, cram it under crumpled up lists of the February sales contests. Please, God, let the garbage man come before this starts to smell rancid. Please please pretty please...

I am scared by the exhilaration that comes with knowing that my sandwich is safely stowed in the garbage. Heart twisting, I know the sin in what I just did. I try not to care. I can't not care. But still the sandwich rots.

Recovery? What's that?

Hands tremble. Steady, girl. Keep moving. Don't think about it. Just don't think. It's okay. Okay?

Focus on your job. Can't you do *anything* right? Weakling, needing to be fed like an animal at the zoo. Walrus chin. Buffalo arms. Hippo ass. Kangaroo stomach. Elephant thighs.

I smile at another customer, make up yet another story about how gosh darn *happy* I am. I wonder whether she may have eaten less than me. She couldn't have had less at lunch—could she? I mentally arrange all of the Build-a-Bear Workshop employees into two categories: thin and fat. I place myself in the latter. I weigh a maximum of 105 pounds. Once I get below 100, I can call myself thin. Then I'll be happy. Just five pounds. That's all. Promise. Five more teensy-weensy pounds between me and thin.

I scurry into the bathroom, inspect my makeup in the mirror and reapply my lipstick. Examine the gut. Sticks out, as usual. Ditto for the butt.

I overhear two other employees discussing cookies. I nearly drool in anticipation. Fat whore, always wanting Mrs. Field's, fresh from the oven. I whisper a hex on those skinny people who can eat sweets. I am painfully conscious of the fact that I'm not one of them.

My stomach growls a token protest. I swig down some cold water. Heart beats a fast little pittery pat in my chest, then slows. Pride. Relief. I didn't break down and eat. Did you hear that everyone? I DIDN'T EAT!

No one answers. They usually don't.

CR

The fact that you were essentially dead does not register until you begin to come alive.
Frostbite does not hurt until it starts to thaw. First it is numb. Then a shock of
pain rips through the body. And then, every winter after, it aches.
And every season after is winter, and I do still ache.

Marya Hornbacher, Wasted

Sadness descends, a wrenching pain as my spirit is removed. What words can I use to describe nothingness? Silence. My cuts and scratches speak for me, vibrant illustrations of depression and fear, rage and tears. Picasso never drew as great as me with my razor. My canvas is my skin; blood, my paint. Showers are an extra-special bonus, the burn as each jet of water strikes the raw skin. Warm now, swelling, macrophages rushing to the scene. Cover the evidence with flannel pajama pants, no Band-Aids required. My little secret. Oh, yes—all mine. And you cannot take it away from me. To think that all I did was pick at my toes—what fools. Just a scratch or two or ten to warm my skin, dull my pain. Razors do a much better job than nail clippers or therapy.

a cut above
razor
thin sharp
honed to perfection
shaves a whisker
nicks the skin: red
blood oozes from the tiny
cut
flesh held together
now breaking apart
and all the life spills out
until a Band-Aid is applied
and the wound scabs over

I take the blade into my hands, caress the cool metal. Making sure the door is locked, I center the razor over my bare thigh. Set the blade in place, press gently but firmly, pull. Watch the skin split, blood pooling into the deep abyss, that deep, dark hole where all feelings go. Pain. Slash. Nothing. Anger. Frustration. Disappointment. Slash. Nothing. The cuts make everything go away; it's just me and the blood and the split second of pain before my skin, too, becomes numb. My brain begins to focus, notes the number of seeping wounds. I clean myself off, patch my leg up, and the only sign there was ever anything wrong is the raised angry marks on my leg. You can still see the marks of pain long past, those faint pink lines barely noticeable in the field of skin.

ॐ

No one warned me about the strange aftermath of an eating disorder, the point in time when you are done with it, but it is not yet done with *you*. No one warned me about the shattered dreams, the wounded body and soul, the hurts and scrapes and sores that sting madly as they are cleansed. I had no idea anorexia would lead me to two different hospitals, to a treatment center halfway across the country, to a toilet bowl, to a razor blade. I can only imagine the trajectory of my life had I not discovered the monster in the mirror.

On good days, I'm able to see that recovery is a wonderful adventure, a discovery of the person I am deep down inside. I have smothered myself for so long that I am no longer even sure of what makes me tick. I am only aware of what enables me to face each day without the crutch of an eating disorder. I am now learning all sorts of things about myself: that my favorite color is green, that I have an affinity for all things Celtic and celestial, and that I can wallow in the sloppy joy of a PB & J sandwich made by an equally sloppy seven-year-old. I am starting to learn that smiles and puppy dogs and grinning chins dripping ice cream on the upholstery are more important than a number on a scale ever will be. I know that Hallmark doesn't make cards that say, "Congratulations, you look like you just escaped from (insert name of concentration camp here)!", nor would any of my friends have sent me one. I see now that people were not designed to subsist solely on mustard and celery sticks, though I still try, against all odds, to believe I can.

The voice I hear in my head—my alter ego, best friend, and worst critic, the one who still tries to convince me that lettuce is a food group—is a liar. She promises she'll let me eat after I lose five more pounds. She says I'll find joy if I do. But I never found it before, I protest. Still, I go on believing her because to do otherwise would admit defeat, and I am too damned stubborn to accept that. Helga and I shared a skull for more than a decade. Before, I obeyed her every command, terrified she would find me wanting. Now? I ignore her and let her yammer on mindlessly, because she is not real, while I am. After a bit, she usually runs out of things to say. It's much quieter in my head now.

The silence, though, leaves a vast ocean of emptiness that no amount of distractions can fill. I try. God knows I try. Every possible bad coping mechanism suggests itself, and I begin to wonder what the hell the Meaning of it All is anyway, how on earth I am going to survive without her. My eating disorder filled a very real void in my life, and I still grieve for its loss.

April 2002

I ate a slice of cheese. Provolone.

It was my first piece of cheese in nearly a year and a half, a half-hearted attempt at normalcy in a life that had become profoundly abnormal. Mind racing, I scanned the menu for their "heart healthy" options. Chicken club, BLT, tuna, roast beef reuben, smoked turkey and provolone. What the hell was *wrong* with these people? Didn't they know that these sandwiches were *loaded* with *fat*? Heart healthy, my ass.

Should I skip lunch altogether and leave without ordering? Or order it without the cheese and dressing? Will they think I'm neurotic?

The pounding of my heart drowned out the din of clinking silverware. Dressing or cheese. Pick, damn you, pick! I swallowed. Which of these has less fat? Cheese or dressing?

I ate the slice of cheese.

I wolfed my sandwich down, horrified that someone might see me eating, desperate to get this ordeal over with. Specters of the damage I have wrought upon my arteries danced in my head. I imagined little curds of half-digested cheese racing toward my hips, a contest to see who can get there first. My brain nearly exploded with the shrapnel of racing thoughts storming through my consciousness. Was it really okay to eat cheese? I mean, really *really* okay, or just kind of okay? Do the people in the restaurant think I am fat? They must— I ordered provolone. It was a bloody slice of *cheese*, for the love of God. Cheese is for fat people.

What had I *done*?

I drove home, trying to outrace the fat hitchhiking home on my butt.

CR

What am I hungry for?

I ask myself this question every day, several times a day, in fact, as I stand in front of the refrigerator and ogle the smorgasbord chilling in front of me. What do I want? What do I *want*?

At least now I am allowed to want.

Women have become experts at reigning in the pull of desire, the throb of appetite that continually rises up and threatens to consume us whole. We don't know what to do with our appetites, since society doesn't even acknowledge they exist. So what *do* we do with them? Deny them, deny we're hungry or lonely or unfulfilled? In doing so, we deny our appetite for life. Anorexia is very much like the Land of the Living Dead. We are as close to dead as you can possibly get—physically, mentally, spiritually. Learning how to nourish myself revived me, brought me back from the dead.

I want *that*.

It's revolutionary.

People who subsist on fewer than twelve hundred calories per day are medically considered to be starving themselves. At the height of my eating disorder, I was consuming a maximum of two hundred and fifty calories per day, the rough equivalent of two and a half slices of bread.

Let me put it in perspective for you. At Treblinka, the Nazis considered the lowest subsistence diet to be nine hundred calories per day. I was eating less than *one-third* of what the Nazis fed to a group of people they systematically rounded up and murdered. No one begrudged Timothy McVeigh his last supper of mint chocolate chip ice cream, yet I refused to allow myself any small gratification.

To quote Sara, "If I did to you what you did to you, I would be in prison."

She is, of course, completely correct.

Anne Lamott writes of her recovery from bulimia:

> But when I feel fattest and flabbiest and most repulsive, I try to remember that gravity speaks; that no one needs plastic-body perfection from women of age and substance. Also, that I do not live in my thighs or in my droopy butt. I live in joy and motion and cover-ups. I live in the nourishment of food and the sun and the warmth of the people who love me.... Learning to eat was about learning to live—and deciding to live; and it is one of the most radical things I've ever done.[15]

ନ୍ଧ

"I'm just going out for a quick bike ride," I called out, as the screen door swung shut behind me and I buckled on my helmet. "I'll be back in half an hour."

On an unusually warm day in mid-April, I set out in shorts and a T-shirt. I didn't make it very far. I don't really have many memories of what happened once I left my driveway—one minute I was pedaling, then my legs started spasming, then everything went black and the ground swallowed me up as my bike crashed onto the shoulder of the road. My parents thought I had been hit by a car when they were called to the scene by the shrill whine of the ambulance sirens. Someone helped my rigid-yet-still-convulsing unconscious body to its feet, legs twitching one last time before they, too, became still. My mom rode in the ambulance with me, filled out a health history form. The medic made a special note of my history of anorexia. I proceeded to spend

---

[15]*Traveling Mercies*, Pgs. 197-198

the evening in the ER, trying to convince the doctors that I wasn't overheated, I wasn't dehydrated. "I hardly made it a thousand feet beyond the end of my driveway. I didn't have *time* to get dehydrated. And it wasn't even that hot." They nodded their heads and said "Mmmm-hmmm." I knew they didn't believe me.

We didn't know what it was then. In fact, we would have no idea until the same thing happened again, only this time I was in an elevator, moving into my new apartment in Ann Arbor. And this time, when everything went black, my chest was paralyzed and I stopped breathing. My face turned pink… red… purple… blue. My mother yelled, "I think we're losing her, Doug! God, I think we're losing her!" Another call to 911 by a stranger. I finally started to come out of it, rigid muscles finally relaxing. This time, we learned something from our trip to the ER—my disorder had a name. Epilepsy.

Seizures, and seizure disorders like epilepsy, are still a mysterious phenomenon, known to be caused by any number of different factors. One of the most common threads is, however, some kind of injury to the brain, some kind of brain damage.

Brain damage.

It suddenly hit me—brain damage. My God…

Starvation is known to cause brain damage.

Was I really that sick?

I thought I had emerged from anorexia completely unscathed. My osteoporosis was reversing itself, I was no longer hooked on black coffee and Diet Coke, and I was eating, functioning, doing well.

But the body never forgets. Never completely. And now I have a Medic Alert bracelet on my left wrist that serves as a constant reminder of the cost of anorexia.

ՑՅ

I have yet to meet a person with anorexia who hasn't, at some time or another, viewed recovery as selling out to his or her beloved mistress. We are betraying her, somehow, by getting better, by moving on with our lives. All this for a disease that is trying to kill us. But the equation also works like this—she, in some sense, needs us as much as we need her. Without our adoration, she simply dries up, crumbles into dust, and is blown away in the wind. Each recovered person that walks around in this world, head held high, is one more stroke of the blade that kills this she-demon that haunts so many.

An eating disorder is very much like a living, breathing entity. And this life form has gotten rather good at festering in small sores, at spreading from person to person with a single glance, a single comment. When recovery breaks this chain of transmission, anorexia has to adapt and find some new way to pass itself on, or she will die. By examining an eating disorder like the potently live, dangerous disease it is, it makes sense that anorexia does not want to die. To keep this from happening, anorexia convinces us that we want her, we need her, in order to do even menial tasks like brushing our teeth and combing our hair. She tries to ensure that we never abandon her by laying a phenomenal guilt trip upon our bony shoulders should we even consider breaking the contract that we so naively signed—You give me love and adoration and I, Anorexia, will make you skinny. By these devious, deceitful means, anorexia keeps herself alive.

So, you might ask, do I want to live or not? The answer for the time being is obvious. I am writing this, so I must have chosen life, at least on some level. My urges both to self-destruct and to live are at a precarious balance, a balance that could tip either way, but nevertheless a balance that allows me to face each day. When I actually sit down and think about it, I have no intention of going back.

Have I discovered the reason to go on living? No. My life is still out there, and I know the purpose will come. I have the most marvelous opportunity to choose what I want to do with my life, a luxury not afforded to many people. Who am I to waste it on choosing how small my jeans will be? I might never win the Nobel Prize in Physiology, but that's the sorriest reason I've ever heard for starving myself to death.

I want my life back. That simple statement has sustained me through all of the gas and bloating, the constipation, night sweats, and mood swings.

I.

Want.

My.

Life.

Back.

I used to take pride in having people know I was anorexic—how little I ate, how thin I was, how long I exercised, how many laxatives I took. Now I'm working not to let on that I ever had an eating disorder. I want to be as normal as possible. The only way I want people to find out I once ventured into the hellish world of anorexia is if I tell them. And it takes time. That's the hardest thing to learn. Just as we wanted to be thin *now*, we want to be better *now*. But it's not that simple.

Although I have managed to learn many important things from my experience with anorexia, I wouldn't wish an eating disorder upon anyone. I would rather have these lessons been taught more gently, so that I didn't get a year's hiatus from college and, indeed, life itself. Anorexia has invariably changed me, forcing me to decide whether I wanted to live or die. The choice was simple math—the price for remaining skeletal was more than I was willing to pay. I will live the rest of my life with the knowledge that going back is only a few easy steps away, that I can lose the weight any old time I want. Empowerment is not starving an already wasted body; it's knowing that I can stop eating, but choosing instead to pick up my fork and take one goddamned bite after another. As much as I still desire to lose just five more pounds, I have come to realize that the price is just too high, and that being thin is not worth a life devoid of all life.

> *And when I chose to live,*
> *There was no joy, it's just a line I crossed.*
> *Wasn't worth the pain my death would cost,*
> *So I was not lost—*
> *Or found.*

Dar Williams, "After All"

I wish I could come to the point where I could say, that's it. That's my story. But life doesn't work that way. There are no fairy-tale endings concocted by Hollywood producers, not here. I have inherited a brain on the fritz, plunging into obsessions and compulsions one day, and seizures the next. My body is still weakened, so that at the first sign of malnutrition, it shuts down and I start shivering and trembling like before. But compared to many, I am lucky. You can look at me now and never know that I once reduced myself to merely a skeleton.

As I write this, I cannot claim that I am totally recovered, but I have faith that one day, I will be able to declare that I am. For now, I simply wake up each morning and take another tentative step away from my eating disorder, and each evening it gets harder and harder to comprehend turning back to anorexia.

There are many things an anorexic will learn in recovery:

You will learn that giving up recovery and turning back to anorexia is much easier than pushing forward, though it always seems the other way around. You will learn that death is a cop-out. You will eat a slice of watermelon and taste summer; you will sip a cup of hot cocoa and wallow in the howling snow outside your window. You will learn that life is lived in the small moments, in the voices of our friends and the laughter of children. You will learn that life has its ups and downs, but you would rather take the worst of life without anorexia than the best days of your life as an anorexic. Regardless of how shitty your day may be going, you will come to understand that *you can handle it just fine*. Without the help of an eating disorder.

I have learned that time heals all wounds. Maybe not completely, maybe not perfectly, maybe not right away, but Father Time does smooth over the jagged, torn skin until your gaping cut is no more than a pink, puckered scar. Scars bestowed upon me by Helga still litter my spirit; their more corporeal counterparts remain scattered over my thighs from Helga's aftermath. The only other visible scar remaining on my body is on my ankle: a recent fall shattered my brittle, osteoporosis-ravaged bones. I am put back together like Humpty-Dumpty, plates and screws keeping my foot attached to my leg. The surgery is visible, though the hardware is not. All that you see is a bright pink puckered line disappearing into my shoe.

It is, however, the invisible scars that plague me the most. The ones concealed beneath layers of flesh, deep down in my soul. The ones that live in that terrible world of what should have been. The blank scrapbook pages. The roads not taken. Yet strange as it sounds, I'm beginning to like my scars, visible and otherwise. They are my history. They are me.

I have filled my gas tank, so to speak. I am no longer running on empty; indeed, my tank runneth over. I have family, friends, a job, an education, things to live for. I have refueled, and it is time to take that car out for a spin and see where she may go.

I hope to see you there.

Cast me gently into morning
for the night has been unkind.
Take me to a place so holy
That I can wash this from my mind
The memory of choosing not to fight.
If it takes a whole life I won't break I won't bend
It'll all be worth it, worth it in the end.

Sarah McLachlan, "Answer"

We are each the hero of our own story.

Mary McCarthy

Epilogue: Pomp and Circumstance
May 2002

It is finally here. Graduation and commencement. I hear my name called, the quiet reverberations from the loudspeakers. Despite the numerous predictions to the contrary, my turn has come and I am walking across that stage and shaking those hands and receiving my degree. Right or wrong, this is my moment. I will not share it with Anorexia. I have made it in spite of her, and I have made it specifically *to* spite her.

The moment, in all its glory, is bittersweet. People talk of the fun of their college years and I laugh right along with them. Inside, I am thinking of the days spent without food, the sleepless nights endured, the workload from hell. The raging flow of memories floods my brain, a tempestuous river of endless pictures in the scrapbook of my consciousness. Ah, yes, college… that was when I thought five baby carrots were a meal. That was when I was so hungry I ate leftovers out of the garbage. That was when my soul shriveled up and I almost blew away in the breeze.

What hurts the most is knowing that I am the only person responsible for this, that I sabotaged my own happiness for the sake of a couple of measly numbers. In an irony that never fails to astound me, I am never proud of these figures in and of themselves. Instead, they represent a need overcome, an urge conquered, a rebellion quelled. What else can I say—that I starved myself down to eighty-five pounds and lived as a reclusive workaholic? That I managed to live for several months on black coffee and Life Savers? That I should be dead but, somehow, miraculously, I'm not?

In the end, what does all of this prove? I could blather on for several more pages about my woes and regrets, but it gets me precisely nowhere. Rather than spending the rest of my life lamenting what could have been, or trying to make up for all the lost time, I have instead decided to make the best of the time I have left. I don't want to gloss over the hell or the pain, but neither do I want to wallow in despair. It gets singularly boring after a while. Life goes on. Time marches steadily forward, carrying me along with it, because I'm letting it. I can never go back to being the same person I was before anorexia took over. But I am much stronger and surer of myself now, a woman grown compared to a gawky adolescent girl. The irony of this whole ordeal is that anorexia was the only thing that could have made me strong enough to defeat it.

And so, on my graduation day, I taste my first few breaths of freedom, inhale the crisp sweetness of the morning air, letting it expand my lungs. I recall the sharp pain of the journey, comparing it to the softness of my present existence. I look at how far I have yet to go and how far I've come, the struggle I endured to get to where I am right now. I ask myself if recovery was worth it, if each precious day of peace on the other side of the looking glass was worth the incessant battle to arrive there.

It is. Oh, it is.

Acknowledgements

A hearty kudos goes out to the staff at the Westacres branch of the West Bloomfield Public Library for putting me in touch with many of the scholarly works I consulted while writing this book. They never once batted an eyelash at my numerous strange requests for rather esoteric literature, and managed to track down every title I gave them.

To my treatment team, for quite simply saving my life and helping me find my way back from the hellish world of an eating disorder, and also for simply knowing when I needed a good kick in the ass. This includes, but is not limited to Anne Edwards, Ph.D., Susan Gottleib, Ph.D., Patrizia Jesue, R.D., Susan Catto, M.D., and Alexander Sackeyfio, M.D. Thanks also to staff at Rogers Memorial Hospital, the Renfrew Center of Philadelphia (yes, Gertie, even *you*...), and Beaumont Hospital.

To the wonderful, amazing people at First Page Publications, for showing me that dreams really do come true. You've been more like family than publishers. Thanks to Joe, Marian, Sarah, Meredith, Kim and Victoria.

To Gary Weisserman for first telling me I should go be a writer, and to Natalie Dykstra for telling me I had to drop everything and write this book.

To Sara, for always putting up with me, and, perhaps more importantly, for knowing when not to.

To Elizabeth, dearest Liz, for her amazing strength that comes from gentleness and love, and for believing in me and standing by my side when the days grew bleak and dim.

To my friends, the whole strange and wacky crew of you, for reminding me why I'm fighting this battle in the first place. To Julie, for never letting me cut the ties that bound us together, and for working with me on our *Anchor* pages, week after week, at all hours of the night and never once losing her temper with me. To Sherri, for a continual source of caffeinated conversation. To Amy, for using herself as an example to show me what life was like on the other side of an eating disorder.

To my Uncle Rob, for showing me how to pull myself up from rock bottom, and for reminding me why you never give up. I know you don't think so, but you are an inspiration.

To all those brave men and women who paved the way for me on the path to recovery, shared their uplifting stories, and reminded me what was waiting for me on the other side. I can't thank you enough for your inspiration and boldness where most fear to tread. Thanks especially to Kyrai Antares for reminding me that the problem was never with myself and that there is nothing wrong with me.

I mustn't forget my cat, Aria, and her remarkable ability to find the exact spot I am working on in the manuscript and plunk her furry rump right down on top of it.

Lastly, to my parents, for always letting me read at the dinner table, for never giving up on me, for always believing I could do It (whatever It may be), for putting up with my mood swings and crabbiness on my way to gentler waters, and for incessant hours of support and love. Thank you, thank you, and thank you again.

Bibliography

Antares, Kyrai. *Finding a Break in the Clouds: A Gentle Guide and Companion to Breaking Free from an Eating Disorder.* Victoria, Canada: Trafford Publishing, 2001.

Baer, Lee. *Getting Control: Overcoming Your Obsessions and Compulsions.* New York: Plume, 2000.

———. *The Imp of the Mind: Exploring the Silent Epidemic of Obsessive Bad Thoughts.* New York: Plume, 2002.

Bell, Rudolph. *Holy Anorexia.* Chicago: University of Chicago Press, 1985.

Bordo, Susan. *Unbearable Weight: Feminism, Western Culture, and the Body.* Berkeley, CA: University of California Press, 1995.

Boskind-White, Marlene and William C. White, Jr. *Bulimia/Anorexia: The Binge/Purge Cycle and Self-Starvation.* New York: W. W. Norton, 2001.

Brown, C. and K. Jasper, eds. *Consuming Passions: Feminist Approaches to Weight Preoccupation and Eating Disorders.* Ontario, Canada: Second Story Press, 1993.

Bruch, Hilde. *Conversations with Anorexics.* (posthumous). D. Czyzewski and M. Suhr, editors. New York: Basic Books, 1988.

———. *The Golden Cage: The Enigma of Anorexia Nervosa.* Boston: Harvard University Press, 2001.

Brumberg, Joan Jacobs. *Fasting Girls: The History of Anorexia Nervosa.* New York: Vintage Books, 2000.

———. *The Body Project: An Intimate History of American Girls.* New York: Vintage Books, 1998.

Butler, Judith. *Gender Trouble.* New York: Routledge, 1990.

Chernin, Kim. *The Obsession: Reflections on the Tyranny of Slenderness.* New York: HarperPerennial, 1994.

———. *The Hungry Self: Women, Eating, and Identity.* New York: HarperPerennial, 1994.

———. *Reinventing Eve: Modern Woman in Search of Herself.* New York: HarperPerennial, 1994.

Claude-Pierre, Peggy. *The Secret Language of Eating Disorders: How You Can Understand and Work to Cure Anorexia and Bulimia.* New York: Vintage Books, 1998.

Contiero, Karen and Wendy Lader. *Bodily Harm: The Breakthrough Healing Program for Self-Injurers.* New York: Hyperion, 1999.

Costin, Carolyn. *The Eating Disorder Sourcebook: A Comprehensive Guide to the Causes, Treatments, and Prevention of Eating Disorders.* New York: Contemporary Books, 1999.

Edut, Ophira and Rebecca Walker, eds. *Body Outlaws: Young Women Write About Body Image and Identity.* Seattle: Seal Press, 2000.

Fallon, Patricia, Melanie A. Katzman, and Susan C. Wooley, eds. *Feminist Perspectives on Eating Disorders.* New York: Guilford Press, 1994.

Findlen, Barbara, ed. *Listen Up: Voices from the Next Feminist Generation.* Seattle: Seal Press, 1995.

Foucault, Michel. *History of Sexuality, Vol. 1.* New York: Vintage Books, 1990.

Garfinkel, Paul and David Garner. *Anorexia Nervosa: A Multidimensional Perspective.* New York: Brunner/Mazel, 1982.

Garrett, Catherine. *Beyond Anorexia: Narrative, Spirituality, and Recovery.* Cambridge, UK: Cambridge University Press, 1999.

Gordon, Richard. *Eating Disorders: Anatomy of a Social Epidemic.* 2*nd* ed. Oxford, UK: Blackwell Publishers, 2000.

Hall, Lindsey and Monika Ostroff. *Anorexia Nervosa: A Guide to Recovery.* Carlsbad, CA: Gurze Books, 1999.

Hall, Lindsey. *Full Lives: Women Who Have Freed Themselves from the Food and Weight Obsession.* Carlsbad, CA: Gurze Books, 1993.

Hendricks, Jennifer. *Slim to None: A Journey Through the Wasteland of Anorexia Treatment.* New York: McGraw-Hill Books, 2003.

Hesse-Biber, Sharlene. *Am I Thin Enough Yet?: The Cult of Thinness and the Commercialization of Identity.* New York: Oxford University Press, 1996.

Hornbacher, Marya. *Wasted: A Memoir of Anorexia and Bulimia.* New York: HarperPerennial, 1999.

Johnson, Anita. *Eating in the Light of the Moon: How Women Can Transform Their Relationship With Food Through Myths, Metaphors, and Storytelling.* Carlsbad, CA: Gurze Books, 2000.

Kano, Susan. *Making Peace with Food: Freeing Yourself from the Diet/Weight Obsession.* New York: Harper & Row, 1989.

Kilbourne, Jean. *Can't Buy My Love: How Advertising Changes the Way We Think and Feel.* New York: Free Press, 2000.

Knapp, Carolyn. *Appetites: Why Women Want.* New York: Counterpoint Press, 2003.

Lerner, Betsy. *Food and Loathing: A Lament.* New York: Simon and Schuster, 2003.

Maine, Margo. *Body Wars: Making Peace with Women's Bodies.* Carlsbad, CA: Gurze Books, 2000.

———. *Father Hunger: Fathers, Daughters and Food.* Carlsbad, CA: Gurze Books, 1991.

Malson, Helen. *The Thin Woman: Feminism, Post-structuralism, and the Social Psychology of Anorexia Nervosa.* London: Routledge, 1998.

Orbach, Susie. *Hunger Strike: Starving Amidst Plenty.* New York: Other Press, 2001.

Newman, Lesléa, ed. *Eating Our Hearts Out: Personal Accounts of Women's Relationship to Food.* Freedom, CA: The Crossing Press, 1995.

Penzel, Fred. *Obsessive-Compulsive Disorders: A Complete Guide to Getting Well and Staying Well.* New York: Oxford University Press, 2000.

Rabinor, Judith Ruskay. *A Starving Madness: Tales of Hunger, Hope, and Healing in Psychotherapy.* Carlsbad, CA: Gurze Books, 2002.

Rhodes, Constance. *Life Inside the "Thin" Cage: A Personal Look Into the Hidden World of the Chronic Dieter.* New York: Shaw Books, 2003.

Roth, Geneen. *When You Eat at the Refrigerator, Pull Up a Chair.* New York: Hyperion, 1998.

Sacker, Ira M. and Mark A. Zimmer. *Dying to be Thin: Understanding and Defeating Anorexia Nervosa and Bulimia—A Practical, Lifesaving Guide.* New York: Warner Books, 1987.

Sandbek, Terence J. *The Deadly Diet: Recovering from Anorexia and Bulimia, 2nd ed.* Oakland, CA: New Harbinger Publications, 1993.

Seid, Roberta. *Never Too Thin: Why Women Are at War with their Bodies.* New York: Prentice Hall, 1991.

Shanker, Wendy. *The Fat Girl's Guide to Life.* New York: Bloomsbury USA, 2004.

Siegel, Michelle, Judith Brisman, and Margot Weinshel. *Surviving an Eating Disorder: A Guide for Family and Friends.* New York: Perennial Books, 1997.

Solomon, Andrew. *The Noonday Demon: An Atlas of Depression.* New York: Simon and Schuster, 2002.

Wand, Marilyn. *Fat! So? Because You Don't Have to Apologize for Your Size.* New York: Ten Speed Press, 1999.

Way, Karen. *Anorexia Nervosa: A Hunger for Meaning.* New York: Harrington Park Press, 1996.

Weiner, Jessica. *A Very Hungry Girl: How I Filled Up on Life and How You Can, Too.* New York: Hay House, 2003.

Wilson, Reid and Edna B. Foa. *Stop Obsessing! How to Overcome Your Obsessions and Compulsions.* New York: Bantam, 2001.

Wolf, Naomi. *The Beauty Myth: How Images of Beauty are Used Against Women.* New York: Anchor Books, 1992.

Zerbe, Kathryn L. *The Body Betrayed: A Deeper Understanding of Women, Eating Disorders, and Treatment.* Carlsbad, CA: Gurze Books, 1995.